6th Edition (updated for re-release 2022)

Foreword

"One of the most important principles of success is –
Developing the habit of going the extra mile."
Napoleon Hill

I met **Bob Hooey** personally for the first time in 2009 at the Canadian Association of Professional Speakers annual convention in snowy Calgary. I was attending the convention in my role as the International President of the Global Speakers Federation. We got to know each other better when Bob was keynoting the PSA Holland convention that next spring and later at other speaker conventions and visits.

I had been following Bob from afar on Facebook and LinkedIn for some years and loved his positive attitude and outlook. But, more importantly I loved his prolific writing and information on business building and customer service.

When we met, I realized we had similar ideals and values around the things that matter in business; one of which is good customer service. Like Bob I'm passionate about good service and was thrilled when he asked me to write a few words as the foreword of the fifth edition of this book.

I think we have all experienced both good and bad service in our personal lives and business dealings and travels around the world. Nothing can make or break an experience more than a memorable service moment. Remember though, memorable can be positive or negative.

The simple use of a person's name in a customer service interaction can turn the 'mundane' into a special moment. One of my most memorable yet simple moments like this was after boarding a Qantas International Flight on a Boeing 747. An average 747 holds somewhere between four to five hundred passengers and is obviously split into different cabins, with first class, business, and economy passengers.

This particular flight was full, with not a spare seat in sight. I was flying in the economy cabin and the same flight attendant who greeted me at the cabin door on boarding was serving the meals in the cabin where I was seated. When she arrived at my seat, she said brightly *"Hello again Mr. Adams, would you like the chicken or beef tonight?"*

I have to tell you, I nearly fell off my seat; she not only remembered my name, she used it in our conversation and made me feel so welcome. A simple moment, turned into a memorable customer service experience.

As an international conference speaker and author, I'm always on the lookout for stories to tell to illustrate the points I make in my presentations and my writing. In *'Make ME Feel Special!' The Art of Customer Service*, Bob uses the same method to enhance his theories and perspectives on customer service. As an in-demand speaker he has travelled the world and collected an armory of practical tips, tools, and ideas that he shares throughout the book.

Bob is a prolific author and has written over thirty books on leadership, sales, presentation skills, and, of course customer service. In a previous life, Bob owned and managed a kitchen design business, selling and making kitchens for homeowners in Edmonton and Calgary, Alberta and later in Vancouver, BC. He honed his customer service and sales skills working with prospective customers and happy clients who became repeat buyers and raving fans of his quality kitchens. I believe this is where Bob developed the foundation for many of his theories and techniques that he writes about in this book.

Like all good researchers though, Bob has since tested and retested his theories in his professional speaking business and with clients who hire him to help their organizations and their teams deliver better customer service.

In this sixth edition, Bob has updated sections relating to social media and relationship building and has substantially updated the customer service examples to enable the book to keep pace with today's approach to service. Like so many books today, *'Make ME Feel Special!'* is available in good old fashioned paperback, electronically on Kindle and other platforms, as well as when Bob is speaking.

Lindsay Adams, CSPGlobal
2009-2010 President, Global Speakers Federation
Life Member, Nevin Award Winner, Past National President, National Speakers Association of Australia
President, VSAI 2022
www.lindsayadams.com

Preface

Dedicated to our 'Clients', who may choose, at times, to be our 'Customers'

As you delve into *'Make Me Feel Special!'* you might notice we have used the word 'client' here and there in this publication on *'Idea-rich customer service strategies'*, in some cases, using both 'client/customer'. This is a deliberate choice in our vocabulary and a foundational change in mindset we feel necessary to help you enhance your chances of attracting and retaining customers who will become your biggest fans and champions (clients).

Business success (whether retail, service-based, or even direct buyer connections) is built on establishing mutually profitable relationships; relationships where you make the customer (client) feel special.

When you *'Make ME Feel Special!'* you enhance your chances of converting me from a one-time customer to a long-term raving client.

Client vs. Customer: Aren't they really the same thing?

Webster's defines these two seemingly interchangeable words

- **Customer:** one that purchases a 'commodity' or service
- **Client:** one that is **'under-the-protection'** of another; a person who engages the professional advice or services of another

---

Ever wondered why the top performing business owners and sales superstars sell so much better and make so much more money than their counterparts? Plus, they seem to it so much easier too. Their secret is in how they 'visualize' and more effectively approach everyone, which results in such higher levels of success with their prospective clients.

- **They see clients** vs. customers walk into their locations and act accordingly.
- **They see clients** when they pick up the phone or walk into an office or boardroom.
- **They see clients** when there is a concern or something that needs to be fixed or replaced and they act with a long-term view.

- **They see clients** who become raving fans and champions for them.

Take a moment and reflect on the underlying 'differences' in the meanings of these two words. The way a person, who does business with you, can be approached and treated will directly impact your results. In the past, you may have referred to them as customers. Please think of them as clients!

When I started writing our successful on-line *'Secret Selling Tips'* issues (2006), we started calling them 'customers' to align with typical retail terminology used by our first client. We transitioned back to 'Clients' with an explanation of our thinking in year two to help them 'change' their viewpoint and culture.

Prior to creating and launching *'Secret Selling Tips'* I had thought of them (customers) as clients. This focus was, in part, from the many years of serving my design 'clients' who came to me for help in creating the kitchen, bathroom, or other room of their dreams. This view was reinforced from connections with leading selling professionals and top performing business owners and managers across North America who shared this mindset.

We've included excerpts from some of our on-line issues as they relate to what we are discussing in *'Make ME Feel Special!'* as a bonus, just for you.

Perhaps it would be a 'profitable' idea for you to follow their lead. The key to this mental shift lies in understanding what **'under the protection'** of another means in your client (customer) interactions.

My thought: This means you don't 'simply' sell someone a service or product 'just' to ensure you make the largest short-term profit or commission possible. You **'serve them best'** by helping them fully explore their options to make the *'best possible choice'* when they purchase something or engage a service from you! You **'serve them best'** by working with them to purchase something that serves their needs from you. We all need to 'sell' to stay in business and this focus is an increasingly important part of the sales/customer service process.

Even if they are not able to clearly articulate what results, products, or services they need; it is important that you, as a top performing professional, work to understand and appreciate exactly what your clients need when they do business with you and your company. The better you do that, the more you will succeed over the long-term. This service or protection mentality also builds solid repeat sales and referral business for you.

When you determine what outcome or benefit is needed (solid qualifying skills), you can gently lead or guide them to that outcome.

You become their solutions provider as well as their trusted guide. When you do, you become a 'high trust' professional advisor/advocate who protects them.

This earned trust builds a foundation for them to remain your client for life and to become your biggest fan. It also builds a foundation for a long-term valuable client friendship. It also allows you to be a productive salesperson.

In our online sales success and print publications we've shared that research shows people 'still' do business with those they trust and like. That research remains true in 2016 and beyond. Keep that in mind as you engage with potential clients.

One of the secrets to business or selling success is to 'maximize' each client relationship by ensuring you demonstrate your 'genuine' commitment to helping them, not just selling them. That mental shift is reinforced when you think of them as 'valued' clients not 'just' customers. The result is they will buy from you again and encourage their friends and contacts to follow their lead in selecting you to serve them. People love to 'buy' but hate being 'sold'.

Leaders, Managers, Owners

We'd suggest this book might be a great reference and discussion guide for you and your team. Work through it and discuss where it is relevant in your specific client interaction and culture. Working to create a client centered culture will pay dividends for years to come. We have *'Make ME Feel Special!'* available as a lower investment E-pub (Kindle) version as well. Why not get each team member their own copy of either the print or E-pub version? If you'd like to make a print bulk order, please contact me and we'll work something out, just for you.
Email: **bob@ideaman.net   www.SuccessPublications.ca**

"In an era when companies see online support as a way to shield themselves from 'costly' interactions with their customers, it's time to consider an entirely different approach: building human-centric customer (client) service through great people and clever technology. So, get to know your customers. Humanize them. Humanize yourself. It's worth it."
    Kristin Smaby, *'Being Human is Good Business'*

Table of Contents

Foreword 2
Preface 4
Table of Contents 7
As we begin… 9
I'm the nice customer…who never comes back! 11
Ideas to get the 'best' use from your copy of 'Make ME Feel Special!' ... 12
What drives you? 14
'Creating Time to Sell' as a part of your 'Make *Me Feel Special!*' journey 15
Unhappy customers cost you money – lots of money! 19
Tell descriptive, idea-rich stories that engage our minds, create value, and help
    sell on more than one level 21
The importance of a professional strategic development plan 24
Observing the speed limits 25
Customers have needs too 27
Conducting an image self-evaluation 28
Finding your ideal client 31
Guess what? 33
Idea-rich Customer Service – An international perspective 34
Master, who is my customer? 36
Idea-rich customer service redefined 37
8 Field-Proven Tips to Increase Your Income 38
Confidence about Credibility 40
What makes 'YOU-nique?' 42
Understanding why people buy… and how I can re-position myself to take
    advantage of that reasoning 43
Killing the 'termites' of BAD or ineffective service 45
The Seven Be-Attitudes of Great Service 50
Friendly works! 52
Are you 'here' to serve me? 53
Asking Great Questions to Qualify Customers 56
Qualifying 'continued' as a crucial step in your success 59
Exploring solutions or Show and Sell 61
How to turn their 'initial' purchase into repeat business 66
How to Up Sell for Increased Sales and Commissions…and to better serve your
    customers 68
Rules of Value-Added Service 70
    Value-added Service – some myths 71
    Value-added Customer Service Solutions 72
Take advantage of growth opportunities 73

Innovate or evaporate – The time to act is NOW!	74
Break-out-of-the-box Thinking	77
Thinking in Reverse to Move Ahead	78
The 10 Pitfalls of Customer Service	79
Five successful techniques for generating increased sales, repeat business, and engaging customers	82
Getting your customers to sell you…Creating fans and champions	85
So you have a problem… that's great!	88
A personal note from Bob	91
Turning Client Complaints into $ and sense!	92
Getting customer feedback using surveys	93
Mistakes Made By Newer (Sales) Staff	95
Creating TIME for effective training	96
Proactive strategies to minimize price objections	100
Checkpoints for Super Sales Techniques	102
Learn to Listen – A forgotten skill for business builders	104
Success Keys from Rubbermaid	111
Service and Teach to Reach!	113
Turning a Winning Proposal into a Loser	115
Bob's B.E.S.T. publications	120
Thanks for reading *'Make ME feel special!'*	122
About the author	123
Copyright and Credits	125
Acknowledgements, credits, and disclaimers	126
Disclaimer	127
What they say about Bob 'Idea Man' Hooey	128
Engage Bob for your leaders and their teams	130

"On very short notice Bob cleared his schedule and graciously presented at our meeting when the original Speaker was unable to attend. **Last week Bob set the tone for our two-day leadership meeting and gave us all a motivational lift.** *His compassion and true interest in people was clearly evident, making him very credible. He shared some great stories, has a wealth of experience and knowledge and it was a pleasure listening to him. His down-to-Earth style makes it easier to retain the information presented. He also followed up with additional info and handouts, cementing his message of building bridges, not walls. Fantastic job, Bob, and thanks again!"*
Barbara Afra Beler, *MBA, Senior Specialist Commercial Community, Alberta North,* **BMO Bank of Montreal**

(Why the green color on front cover? Simply to remind you of money, which comes more readily when you engage in effective idea-rich customer service.)

As we begin...

"Every company's greatest assets are its customers. Because without customers there is no company!"
Michael LeBoeuf

There is a 'retail' component in most forms of business; whether your clients engage a professional service, buy something on-line, or visit a store. Many of the concepts shared here work equally well across lines. Some may be more case specific. As I finish writing the last-minute changes to this updated 6th edition of **'Make ME Feel Special! Idea-rich customer service strategies'**, we continue to expand into an exciting new period in our history. The 21st Century was the beginning of a new Millennium and had some exciting changes to share with us; with even more to come!

Think back to the major changes and advances we've encountered in the past 100 years: putting a man on the moon, the cell phone revolution, personal computers, and the evolution of the Internet, to name just a few! Business has changed with the advancement in technology. New information-based businesses and web-based businesses have been virtually created overnight.

Look at the success of *Google* and *Amazon* for example. Look at the expansion of the web and online apps, products, and services into our everyday and business lives. Internet and faster travel have made us a truly global community. These are just the tips of the coming wave. Are you ready?

Our businesses will be changing rapidly to accommodate and assist the changing needs, desires, and demands of our clients/customers. **Susan Marthaller** counsels us to *"Always think of your customers as suppliers first. Work closely with them, so they can supply you with the information you need to supply them with the right products and services."*

Our staffing issues and training concerns will be challenged, too. How will you equip your staff to effectively deal with the changes you'll experience as you re-invent your company for this exciting new business environment? How will you engage them and generate buy-in as a part of your client / customer service team?

J. Marriot, Jr of the famous Marriot hotel chain shares, *"Motivate them, train them, care about them, and make winners out of them... we know that if we treat our employees correctly, they'll treat the customers right. And if the customers are treated right, they'll come back."* This might be your biggest challenge as well as opportunity.

Our sales process needs to be 'radically' expanded with a client/customer service focus at its core if we are going to grow and successfully compete today. We will use the term **Customer Service / Sales** to remind you of this change in focus. Sales are a solid part of the client / customer service component of your business, and 'both' are the foundation for long-term growth and business success. It is also a profitable art form!

This 6th edition of *'Make ME Feel Special!'* has been updated, rewritten, and enhanced (2022) to serve you better.

When I decided to write for my areas of expertise, I made a conscious decision to go with a workbook format. The rationale behind that decision was a value-added customer service focus. I wanted to keep my books and content current and fresh. I am 'still' learning and want to be able to share new thoughts, new lessons, and new quotes with my audiences and readers.

With the successful advent of **'Print on Demand'** we are now able to convert and/or update our books, workbooks, and e-books into print (available on numerous online retailers) as well as e-pub versions for our readers. This is our 6th publication re-vamped and published in this manner in the past 2 years. Each of them is now available on Amazon in both a print and Kindle version; four of them made it on the best-seller lists, so far. Our e-pub versions are now available on iTunes, Barnes & Noble and other on-line retailers. Our goal is to do this for all our existing publications in addition to writing new ones. We're researching audio book formats for some of them to make it even easier for our readers to access them.

'Make ME Feel Special!' is a work in progress – **Ideas At Work!** I trust you'll like it and find value for you, your staff, and/or your fellow team members in its pages. It is part of our *Idea-rich Legacy of Leadership* series to better equip leaders and their teams. This updated version is my gift to my fellow business owners, leaders, managers, and their staff who work to improve what they offer their clients and to better serve them.

Bob 'Idea Man' Hooey
Author, creative client catalyst
www.SuccessPublications.ca/FeelSpecial.htm for a special bonus
www.SuccessPublications.ca/BusinessSuccess-Tips.html for special business success videos just for you.

I'm the nice customer...
who never comes back!

*"You know me. I'm the nice customer.
I never complain, no matter what kind of service I get.*

I've always found people are just disagreeable to me when I do. Life is too short for indulging in these unpleasant little scrimmages.

I never kid, I never nag, and I never criticize. I wouldn't dream of making a scene as I've seen other people do in public places. I think that's awful. I'm a nice customer.

I'll tell you what else I am. I'm the customer who never comes back. That's my *revenge* for being pushed around.

It's true this doesn't relieve my feelings right off, as telling them what I think of them would – but, in the long run, it's a far more deadly revenge.

In fact, a nice customer like myself, multiplied by others of my kind can just about ruin a business! There are a lot of nice people in the world just like me.

When we get pushed far enough, we go down the street to another store. We shop in places where they're smart enough to hire people who appreciate nice customers.

Together we do them out of millions every year.

I laugh when I see them so frantically spending their money on advertising to get me back, when they could have held my business in the first place with a few words and a smile."

Anonymous (fitting thought isn't it!)

Ideas to get the 'best' use from your copy of 'Make ME Feel Special!'

'Make ME Feel Special!' contains a range of tips, techniques, and ideas to help you improve the way you 'train' and lead your team for shared growth and profitable long-term success with your clients. It evolved into its present format (from a college level program) with the inclusion of stories, ideas, and first-hand experience based on conversations, copious notes, and first-hand observations of productive fellow leaders and retailers. It was made personal from my own experiences in leading and being on a variety of teams across North America and the globe. It is seasoned with my own customer service tips and experiences in retail, direct sales, and professional services.

It has been updated with a focus to assist professionals, owners, and leaders more profitably enhance their business with enhanced customer service. It is designed as a guide for those who want to take personal leadership over their own lives and actions, providing a purpose and making a positive contribution in the lives of their teams and interaction with their clients.

This is <u>not</u> just a book for casual reading. It is a book to be *chewed*, to be dipped into, and leveraged as a resource or reference guide. It is a workbook with provocative questions that help you decide what you want to accomplish with your life, your leadership, and with your client and team relationships. It is your resource, so mark it, highlight it, and make notes in the margins.

To get the best from this book, first visit the Table of Contents to identify which chapters and/or topics meet your most critical, time sensitive needs. Read them carefully and make sure you understand the guidelines and advice given. Some of the topics may not be of direct interest to you (now) depending on your needs. You may wish to read some of the other chapters so that you can understand the needs of other leaders, 'client' or customer service scenarios.

'Make ME Feel Special!' does not contain ALL the answers. It contains a collection of thoughts, notes, clippings, tips, techniques, lessons learned, and ideas shared primarily from one learner, one business leader's (one retailer's) viewpoint, mine. It is simply intended as an aid to your reflection, learning, and inspiration – a resource that you can draw upon. Its aim is to give you a creative resource that, when applied and practiced with your teams, will help you develop and build both your confidence and profitable competence as a leader, manager, and business owner.

A more productive approach would be to take the tips and concepts presented here and blend them with your own leadership style, personality, and creativity. Keep in mind your own time constraints and 'comfort zone' as a leader, business manager, or professional. Generate unique and perhaps personalized ideas on how you can create, give, and improve your interaction and action with your teams.

'Make ME Feel Special!' – 6th **edition** is designed to offer you flexibility in how you leverage it for your personal and professional use.

1) You can easily sit down for an hour or two and read it **cover-to-cover**. This is a great way to start by getting a feel for what is included, especially for newer or emerging leaders, managers, or owners (those who want to take more personal leadership for their lives and better equip their teams to grow) who want to gain the full benefit from their investment.

A word of advice: ***'Make ME Feel Special!'*** is the result of 29 plus years of personal study, first-hand experience, and observation in a variety of leadership, retail, business, and sales roles; as well as coaching and support and coaching roles for executive clients and their respective teams. It might seem overwhelming or confusing at first with the range of information included here. Once you have done a quick read of the whole book, identify sections or tips that interest you and work on manageable chunks.

2) You can select one chapter or section and work to incorporate the ideas you discover into your own specific leadership role, client engagement, or business situation.

3) You can look at the Table of Contents and jump straight to the tips or areas of study that particularly interest you.

We have attempted to incorporate something of benefit for everyone, regardless of your current level or skill in business. You might even find some *contradictory* advice in different parts of the book! ☺ This is because there is no single, universal 'right answer' – you must find what is a right fit for you, your objective, and your team's specific needs. What works for you is what is best. Choose it, try it, and adapt it as needed to serve you in your quest to be a more effective businessperson and impactful leader. Take control of how you allocate, invest, or leverage your time and interaction with your staff and clients. We've written it to help you guide your teams to become more productive and profitably enhance your business dealings with your clients.

What drives you?

"Only a clear definition of the mission and purpose of the business makes possible clear and realistic objectives. It is the foundation for priorities, strategies, plans, and work assignments. It is the starting point for the design of managerial jobs and, above all, for the design of managerial structures." **Peter Drucker**

- What is driving you and your team?
- What is your defined purpose and strategic mission as an organization?
- What are you providing for your prospective clients or customers?
- What are you doing to engage and motivate your team?
- What are you doing to equip yourself and your team to grow and win?

Funny how some non-structured time in the sun with a good book allows your mind to wander and wonder. Amazing how the warmth and sea air can stimulate your imagination and your ability to dream. The end of each quarter is a good time to pause and reflect on how you and/or your team are doing. Remember those goals you set late last year or early this year? Hmmm

I found myself rethinking *'what I do'* and *'why I do it'* on a February trip to Cancun. I had a wonderful time addressing the dealer/owners of a major Canadian National Tire Chain. They were very receptive and open to challenge their own experiences and to revisit *'why'* and *'what'* they were doing. This, I believe, is the beginning of building strong, long-term foundations for profitable success under any organization. Know what drives you help build long-term profitable client relationships.

From personal experience, having a *'strongly defined'*, visual image of your purpose and a strategic mission of what you do will keep you focused. It will also keep you fired up and excited about your business and career. It will help you ride the tough times and challenges that come with everyday life and modern-day business.

My challenge for you is to take a minute... ok, 15 minutes, and take a serious look at what you are doing. **Ask yourself,**

- Why are you doing it?
- What real value do you bring to your industry, market, and clients?
- What are you willing to change to make it better, more attractive, and value-added to your team and your client/customers?

'Creating Time to Sell' as a part of your 'Make *Me Feel Special!*' journey

The *'Creating Time to Sell, Lead, or Manage'* program was originally created and delivered for the BC Management Team of the **St. John Ambulance**, with all their branch managers coming together. The objective for our session was a skillful blending of solid sales, business building, and service principles with a good use of time to allow their respective teams to be more productive in their customer service efforts. It was very well received. We've spent time over the past dozen years refocusing and expanding it as a tool to offer our clients to help them succeed in attracting, profitably selling, and retaining customers and building referral and repeat business.

The secrets and tools we cover in our on-site workshops have allowed top performing professionals, their managers, and their staff to find ways to be more pro-active in 'reaching' and 'retaining' clients for their organizations.

While flying to a speaking engagement in the US, I read a study that indicated the **average salesperson put in a 53-hour week and this might be a low estimate***. Yet, despite this long week,* **less than 8 hours of face-to-face sales activity was recorded (about 15%)***. More recently, I read that the average business owner, leader, or executive had 40-60 hours of unfinished business on their agenda at any one time. Sound familiar?*

I think something is radically wrong with this picture. *Work more and produce less* is not a good indicator for any organization that wants to survive or thrive in an extremely hectic and competitive market. Whatever happened to *'work smarter not harder'*? We are too busy, overwhelmed, and distracted, and that impacts our ability to serve and sell to our clients. We are too busy to invest the necessary time training our staff in their effort to be equipped to succeed. We are too busy to truly enhance our business and generate all the sales potentially available. Sad, really!

To be effective in sales/customer service and business in general, we've been telling our audiences and clients that we must deal with **three areas as they relate to our potential clients.**

- **Pain**
- **Gain**
- **Sustaining**

The degree that you work 'with' your clients/customers to take care of these three areas, will determine the impact on your profitability and long-term viability. Each area has its 'specific focus' and profit center. In the sales process, each area has its impact and effectiveness. At times, we work with clients/customers who have one or more of these areas as their focus. The time we spend finding out what their *'real'* need is increases the likelihood that we will be the one engaged to help solve it.

If we only help people with their **'pain'** – will they 'still' need us when it is gone? What motivation do people have to visit a doctor or dentist when they are feeling well? A word to the wise!

Helping them **'gain'** offers a bit more opportunity to serve and build a profitable long-term business relationship built on repeat purchases.

If you can work with them through their **'pain'**, help them **'gain'** in the process; and then take them through to helping them grow and **'sustain growth'** you will become a major, vital part of their team (business or life) for years to come. That is taking full advantage of leveraging your time in the customer service/sales process for maximum return.

They will deal with you time and again, if you help them see and receive the value you provide. I offer it as a mental jog to focus on using your time more wisely and blend some proven sale principles (I'm sure you've had lots of sales courses) into the mix.

Having said that, how can you focus on the above 3 success focus tools if you are bogged down with minutia and paperwork or are unwisely using your time each day in non-productive, non-sales-oriented activities?

Ask yourself; no, decide to track and analyze exactly how much time you 'actually' spend in the sales/customer service process. The results will surprise you and they may even scare you! Many of us in the sales /customer service field find ourselves easily sidetracked. We spend time doing 'paperwork', filling out reports or 'busy work', chatting on the phone, chatting with our colleagues, reading the paper, taking long breaks, and other such 'non-productive' activities.

Am I saying to eliminate these in their entirety? NO! Simply be aware of where you invest your time – and track the results to ensure that investment is well placed. You **'make money'** in business primarily when you are in face-to-face or phone-to-phone sales or follow up contact with your clients.

You **'earn that money'** by delivering on what you contract and you **'leverage that money'** by good client contact and ongoing service. But first, you need to be and/or keep in contact with them.

- **Prospecting** is good use of time in the sales/customer service process – how much time do you spend doing it? Have you developed a systematic way to track and follow up on each one?
- Have you set-aside specific times each day to contact potential clients? When?
- Have you set aside specific times to maintain contact with existing clients to find out when and where you can help them again? **Repeat sales are the best** and the most profitable ones! *I love it when a client I've spoken for calls and asks me to come again. Referrals don't hurt the process either! Many of my clients hear about me from another client, speaker, or trainer and then call to see if I can help their teams.*
- Have you set aside specific time for follow up, to make sure your current clients received what you promised and are satisfied with their relationship with you?

According to **Marketing Metrics** your probability of selling to existing customers is 60-70% whereas your probability with new prospects is only 5-20%. According to the **White House Office of Consumer Affairs** loyal customers are worth up to 10 times as much as their initial purchase. Factor in, acquiring new clients is 6-7 times more expensive than keeping existing ones and you'll start seeing the value of maintaining good customer service.

Customer service is a success tool for the top performing professional, business owner, and champion salesperson. It amazes them when you call – so few salespeople do! It helps convert them into your champions and fans when you follow-up and ensure they are happy. When you find out early when something is not working correctly or needs adjustment, fix it!

- Have you worked to make it easier for your clients to find you, get the information they need, and track their order or service process? UPS and FEDEX use on-line tracking systems, which is really a very effective sales and marketing tool. **Michael Hammer** drives home the point about being **ETDBW** (easy to do business with) in *'The Agenda'*. Add it to your sales library! How easy are you to do business with?
- We continually evolve our primary website **www.ideaman.net** by expanding and enhancing its different customer driven segments. For example, we've added on-line resources and downloadable articles.

- *My web work is becoming a series of true value-added client-centric sites, as well as very productive and profitable. It is time well spent in creating time to sell, lead, or manage my business and customer contact relationships.*
- Have you 'systemized' your work area and computers to make it easier for you or your colleagues to access information, client files, literature, etc. to better and more quickly serve your clients?
- Have you spent specific time thinking about all the potential challenges or questions that might come up from a prospective client? Have you discussed these challenges and the productive solutions you and your organization provide? Are your staff fully informed and well 'trained' in helping clients with their challenges? Do you have solid, well-researched, value-enhancing answers ready and burned into your mind? Why not?

If you invest even a small amount of time working on these questions and implementing the results of your deliberations – you'll find yourself being able to spend more time on the sales, service, and marketing process. You'll also find you will attract more clients, receive better quality referrals, and garner more profitable repeat business.

Amazingly enough when you are *'Creating Time to Sell, Lead, or Manage'*, as a part of your customer service focus – you end up selling more and making more money too!

Why should you have a mission statement?

Effective mission statements are not so much written on a piece of paper or on a poster but written in the minds and exhibited in the actions of you and your staff. **Ask yourself:**

- Is it something that all your team/staff had input in developing and agree with its aims?
- Is it clear and concise to make it easy to remember?
- Is it visible for customers and staff alike to see while in the work environment? If not, WHY NOT!

"Our mission at Ideas At Work is to profitably provide our clients with field-proven, idea-rich, practical programs in personal and professional effectiveness. (Innovative, engaging programs and materials will enhance their quality of life and advance their careers and effectiveness in their personal, business, or community involvements.)"

Unhappy customers cost you money – lots of money!

Deciding to focus on making your customers feel special can pay off in so many profitable ways, just as 'not taking care' of them can have negative results for you and the survival of your business.

Let me ask you a couple of questions as we move further into our time together.

What is your average sale or transaction worth? (retail) $_____

What is your average cost to gain each sale? (overhead) $_____

Take a moment and discover how much each (average) client or customer generated for you over the past year. For a quick estimate, divide your gross earnings by the estimated client/customer count last year. Take your advertising and other related marketing costs and divide by customer count.

Let's talk about the value of taking care of each of your customers. But first, let's talk about the real cost of having someone 'unhappy' with your services or products.

A variety of research, (e.g., 2011 American Express survey) reveals that:

Unhappy customers tell 10-16 other people about poor experiences, (let's use 10 for an average) whereas Happy customers tell on average 5-9 other people about good experiences (let's use 5 on average)

We contend that each unhappy customer 'costs' your company the purchasing power equal to the minimum purchasing power of 16 customers.

Potential cost of making a customer unhappy is at least 16 lost customers... as follows:

Original customer not returning: 1
Customers lost to sharing 'their' horror story: 10
Customers not gained through positive referrals: 5

Total customer loss = 16 (minimum)

Now how much is each 'unhappy' customer really worth?
16 x $_____ = $ _____

And how much will it take to 'attract' and 'replace' 16 customers?

16 x $ _____ x 6 = $ _____
(Hint: Costs run 6-7 times the annual cost for replacement of a lost client)

Add those two numbers to get a real projection of the value of keeping each customer as a happy client.

Now let me ask you another question. How important is it to train your staff to 'effectively' serve each customer and to be 'empowered' to keep them engaged, happy, and satisfied? (We cover more about this on page 96)

How much is your business worth? Perhaps you see the reason why so many successful stores have liberal return or service satisfaction policies. What changes are needed to make your policies more client friendly?

What changes would you have to make in your training or policies to ensure you satisfy and retain your customer base? What would it be worth to you to see your customers turned into fans and champions - promoting your business around the world? **What is stopping you?**

Happy, engaged clients/customers are the **lifeblood** of any successful business. They don't happen by accident! They are a direct result of your training and promotional efforts and the experience they receive when the meet you face to face or electronically. **Make a commitment today to better serve them!**

Business Building Success Tip

"There are many who subscribe to the convention that service is a business cost; but our data demonstrates that superior service is an investment that can help drive business growth. Investing in quality talent, and ensuring they have the skills, training, and tools that enable them to empathize and actively listen to customers are central to providing consistently excellent service experiences.

Getting service right is more than just a nice to do; it's a must do. American consumers are willing to spend more with companies that provide outstanding service … ultimately, great service can drive sales and customer loyalty." **Jim Bush, Executive VP American Express**

Tell descriptive, idea-rich stories that engage our minds, create value, and help sell on more than one level

Customer service is not 'just' having products or services to sell your clients. It is as much about 'how' you help them experience or investigate potential purchases. It is about being dedicated to helping them make intelligent, value-added decisions that make their life or business better.

Perhaps you've heard or been taught that sharing **Features, Advantages** and **Benefits** is a more effective approach to create 'value' than just feature dumping on our prospective customers or teams. It is! But do we effectively do that in our sales, service, and leadership conversations?

Let me share a simple experience where a young shoe salesman did this very well. We all need shoes and hopefully, since we are on our feet a lot, we select some that are comfortable, yet stylish to wear when we are at work. At least that is my story.☺

A few years back, I was doing some sailing in Puerto Vallarta, Mexico. One afternoon I was enjoying a quiet break doing some window shopping. Along the way, a very stylish, yet simple, pair of two-tone loafers caught my eye in a little shoe store off the quaint cobblestone street. Thinking I was 'only looking'; I stepped into the store to check them out. I picked them up and quickly put them down, as my initial reaction was, *"Wow... they are not cheap!"*

My young and *very wise* shoe expert approached and engaged me in conversation about my visit to his store, to Puerto Vallarta, and what I did for a living. I made the mistake of telling him I was a professional speaker, leadership success coach, and business success trainer who traveled sharing ideas on how others could be more successful in their lives, leadership careers, sales, etc. (Guess he figured I could really afford them... smile.)

Picking up the shoes and holding them with reverent care, he said, *"You know, when you wear these traditional loafers, you're going to have a big smile on your face because 'one of the great things' about these shoes is they're soft calfskin leather with a full leather lining. And, as you wear them, they will mold to the shape of your feet, giving you a 'custom-made' feel."*

He continued, *"It would be fun to walk around in custom-made shoes, don't you think?"*

He could have just said, *"These shoes are all leather, which is flexible, making them very comfortable."* On the surface that sounds good, doesn't it?

However, what he said 'engaged' me and was more effective to get me to seriously consider investing in a pair for myself, don't you think? He was **creating value in my mind.** He talked about how the shoes were made. He mentioned they were bench-crafted, which meant one person was completely responsible for making this specific pair of shoes.

He then went in for the sale, *"Since they are bench-crafted, they have the artisan's name on them. When they're finished, these shoes have no nicks, no scratches, and all the components fit perfectly. Unlike shoes made on an assembly line, these shoes are one of a kind."* Now there is a value proposition if I ever heard one!

Then he asked me a 'simple' closing question, *"What size do you wear?"* He then proceeded to have me slip on a pair in my size.

Feature (which means)	Advantage (which means)	Benefit (to client)
calfskin leather	molds to your foot	custom made feel
full leather lining	finished feel	instant comfort
traditional loafer	will stay in style	wear for years

Long story made short: He was right, they 'are' delightful to wear. When I walked out of his store, both of us had big smiles on our faces. I could hardly wait for the snow to leave back home so I could take them out for a walk here in Northern Alberta. I love them! In fact, I took them to Australia that next January for a walk-about.

Simple story of how one young salesman took 'personal leadership' and leveraged his craft to the next level by engaging his client. He told a story that created 'value' in my mind and allowed me to 'see myself' in those shoes.

Do you do that with your customers when they come into your store? Or when you visit them in their place of business?

Leaders: If you're in a CEO, leadership, or management role, have you done this with those you lead? CEOs and leaders often need to sell ideas and generate buy in from their teams. When their teams see the value, the buy in is much easier to gain. When they buy in, they move on to successfully complete the ideas.

 Visit: **www.SuccessPublications.ca/BusinessSuccess-Tips.html** for special business building success video tips.

Retailers/Business owners: Do you know enough about your services/products/ideas, (for example furniture and electronics dealers), that you craft engaging stories to help your customers see themselves sitting in front of that big screen Plasma TV, on that leather sofa with matching love seat and chair, end tables, coordinated lamps and accents to enjoy that quiet romantic evening together or watching the Super Bowl with friends?

Are you willing to engage your clients (or teams) to help them see it in their mind's eye before they see it in their house, workplace, or place of business?

Do you know enough about your services that you can create captivating stories that help your prospective clients (or teams) see themselves enjoying the benefit of wisely selecting or following you to help enhance their lives, businesses, and careers?

Do you think this might help you build and expand your business or enhance your leadership effectiveness or management career? Get walking and talking.

Visit: www.SuccessPublications.ca/FeelSpecial.htm for special bonus items, just for our readers.

Customer Service superstars are everywhere

I live in rural Alberta and do much of my shopping in nearby Redwater. One place I shop is the local IGA where, owner Ken, always greets me when I drop in. He has trained his staff to be friendly and helpful.

One of the cashiers, Trena, greets me by name.... in fact, she plays with my name and I love it. She say, hi Bob, how are you doing, Bob... etc.

I was in last year before Christmas to get some mixed fruit so my wife, Irene could make hot crossed buns. I looked and couldn't find it on the shelf. I mentioned it to Trena and she took me with her to check the two locations where it might be.... To no avail.

She said, let me see what I can do and came back a few minutes later with a small container she got from the bakery department. Problem solved and the buns were delicious.

People like Trena make you feel special and that is the essence of great customer service. She makes my visits special because she makes me feel special. Perhaps you can follow her example!

The importance of a professional strategic development plan

Whether you are in business for yourself or work for a living, having a strategic plan covering your professional or business development is essential to your long-term success or employability. Failure to plan is truly, as we've heard, planning to fail! **This is particularly important if you want to attract and retain clients and customers.**

A good plan incorporates several basic components:

- A clear definition of the ultimate objective in mind. **Conceive it complete!**
- A good solid foundation built on understanding what is required to make it happen by **doing your homework.**
- An **ACTION** plan with specific goals and objectives tied to specific timelines and checkpoints to make revisions along the way.

How do you define your idea or ultimate objective as it relates to your value-added business or career? A little free flow idea generation or creative, blue sky 'dreaming' works. Ask yourself – some **'what if?'** questions to unlock your creativity and help **unlock your full-service potential.**

- What if I could do anything without fear of failure? I'd _____
- If I had enough money to ensure my basic living for a year, I'd _____
- If I discovered I had talent, could learn the skills I need to: _____ I'd _____

The answers to these types of questions will give you a glimpse into what you'd really like to do; and what may need to change or adapt to get there.

After you've defined your ultimate desire, then what? Well, now it's time to start doing your homework and find out exactly what is needed to make it happen or prepare you to act.

Then comes the fun part – setting specific action plans in place to accomplish goals and objectives that will lead you to your ultimate desire – a whole bunch of happy satisfied customers who love you and tell the world about you! The key here is to ensure that your goals are clear and specific and can be broken down into even more specific objectives.

Any action plan is only as good as its implementation and accountability. This means setting specific timelines for starting and completion of each step. It also means having numerous built-in checkpoints to allow you to monitor your progress and make any fine-tuning adjustments or course corrections to the plan as you move into its implementation.

Are you serious about 'Establishing a Value-added, Customer Service based sustainable business'? INVESTING the necessary time to do some serious thinking about what you want to accomplish, when, and why is essential. Success doesn't come by accident - it requires strategic planning followed by implementation on your ACTION plan.

Observing the speed limits

Most of us, if given enough time to think about it, would be able to determine what truly enriches our lives, what makes us happy, gives us joy and a sense of purpose, or pastes a grin on our chin. **Our problem – we are *'Running TOO Fast'* to even notice**. We're so busy working overtime, meeting deadlines, chasing career opportunities, and running yellow lights that **we don't notice**. The things we value, that bring true riches to our lives, are often lost in the blur.

The hectic pace at which we live is costing us more than we realize; often what we say we value the most! As we crowd each day with more work and activities than it can suitably hold, a heavy penalty is extracted for resisting our impulses to rest. If I can only get this project done, if I can only land this contract, if I can only… then I can rest. As a speaker and author, I am constantly stretched in this area. Left in our wake, amongst the swirling dust, are our friendships, our health, our family, and our connection with our Maker. This is one reason I am so passionate about this topic.

*When I was somewhat younger (teens) I remember saying (after watching my folks and some in their age group in retirement) that **"I'd rather burn out that rust out!"** Boy, was I wrong and arrogant too! That attitude and the speed in which I, like many of my generation, pursued my dreams and careers led me to a premature burn out and the loss of a marriage and a business I loved. A harsh lesson to be learned for not observing the speed limits in my life.*

We are living too fast, and the casualties are piling up along our causeways. Our excessive speeding is having an impact…on our families and those we love most… our kids. **It is killing our communities.**

It is also burning out our workers and **it's killing our businesses**. People hardly have time to stop and talk with their neighbors, colleagues, or clients anymore. Been broken into lately? Ever wonder why no one saw anything? **No one was home!** We were all so busy speeding off to a meeting or to work! This is not conducive to value-added customer service! How can we serve if we are so tired, so overworked, and so spread out? Clients/customers deserve your full attention too!

Slowing down in a speeded-up world is not quitting your career, abandoning your dreams or your desire to provide for your family. Making an impact in this world requires that we slow down at least long enough to focus on the things which matter most and the people we love.

There are times when we simply must grab the wheel, gulp our lattes, and drive. But more importantly, there are times when it is deadly serious to pull over in a rest stop and rest for a while.

Pull over and take a walk to think and reflect on our life and your true destination. Make sure you are heading in the right direction. You may be making good time and progress, but are you working towards a goal that matters to you, that makes sense for your family, and that adds value to your community? So, are you going in the right direction?

Pull over and give that question some thought! Perhaps give *'Running TOO Fast Idea-rich strategies for the overwhelmed'* a read. Learn to create time to lead and still have a life! **(www.SuccessPublications.ca)** You will be glad you did! And so will your customers and fellow workers!

Do you recognize good service when you see it?

I read something recently that mentioned one of the impacts on good customer service is we are not used to recognizing it. Sad, isn't it?

Let's start a customer service revolution! If we want to see our own staff delivering great customer service, perhaps we need to teach them what it is by challenging them to recognize it when they are on the receiving end of it from someone else. If we all start recognizing those who give us great service, it will reinforce it for them as well as ourselves.

If you send me the name of the 'customer service superstar' and their email address, I will send them a free e-copy of this book with a personal note. Perhaps each of us can find a way to acknowledge them.

Customers have needs too

If you are serious about building a successful career and/or sustainable business on the foundations of value-based client or customer service, there are a few areas about customers you may need to know. If you want your clients / customers to receive the best contact with you or want them to be positively impressed with your care and concern for them, read on.

People are unique! Not one of us is the same. We all have different needs. When you meet those needs *'I feel important or special'* and would want you to keep helping me. There are some needs we all share or hold in common. Taking care to ensure you or your business seriously address these needs will build a solid relationship and a successful career or client focused business.

- ***'Make ME Feel Special'* and valued by you.** How do you do this at present? What changes are needed?
- **Make ME feel comfortable with you and not pressured.** Is this how they really feel? What needs to change to meet this basic need and create this type of atmosphere?
- **Give ME your 'undivided' attention and focus.** This is a tough one, but can you do this? How do you discipline yourself so you can do this? Are there training issues or staffing issues that affect this area?
- **Don't judge ME by your perception of my ability to afford what you sell.** How many times have you caught yourself making this judgment? Each person coming into your place of business is a potential customer – if not now, later. **Treat them 'all' specially!**
- **Focus more on ME than your work schedules activities, rules, or personal life.** This is a business killer! How often have you favored your 'policies' rather than quickly responding or dealing with a customer's needs or problem? What needs to change here?
- **Don't ignore ME for someone who appears to be a 'better' prospect.** Have you ever been on the receiving end of this one? How did it feel? What can you do to ensure none of your customers (especially seniors and kids) feel this way?

Just a few areas where being sensitive to the real needs of your customers will help build a good solid relationship. **Bring them back again and again.**

Ask this question, "Would you buy from yourself?" Why? Take the self-evaluation quiz on the following pages and give yourself an honest appraisal.

Conducting an image self-evaluation

"Perception is reality!" This is often the case in our business dealings. People like to deal with people they like or trust. People base their business perceptions on the image we portray. That image is enhanced or blurred by how we act or present ourselves.

Take a moment and give some honest feedback to yourself, based on your past 3 to 6 months' experience in dealing with your clients/customers. Hint: Your answers might lead you to 'unleash' your business potential – and show you where you can improve your client/customer service!

- Is your image one of honesty and straightforward sincerity? How do you know?

- From the buyer's point of view, would you be considered reliable? Why is that true?

- Could you honestly say your customers received special benefits dealing with you not available from one of your competitors? What? Why?

- In their eyes, would you appear to be an expert in your field? Why would they say that?

- Have you been effective in helping solve their problems? How so?

- Would you say you handled complaints to their complete satisfaction? How did you accomplish this?

- Is integrity one of your watchwords? How does it show in your dealings?

- Other than your business dealings, would you think your customers believe you have their best interests and welfare at heart? Why?

- Do your customers look at you as a good reliable source of product or service information? Why?

- Would the majority of your customers continue dealing with your business, even if a competitor offered slightly lower prices? Why would they do that?

- What percentage of your customers or new clients comes from referrals? Why is that number significant?

- How do you plan to keep yourself and your staff educated and current in your field?

- Describe how you keep in touch with past clients. Describe the results.

- Other questions?

If you have been honest in your appraisal of your business operation you might have seen a few areas in which improvement would help. Go back over your answers and **ask yourself,**

- How can I 'unleash' my business potential by improving the answers to this question?

- How can I improve how I seek and service my clients?

- How can I change what I offer them to reflect more accurately what they need?

- How can I make a difference in my career and my community by making the changes I see needed here?

- How can I equip my staff and co-workers to better reflect the changes needed?

- How can I partner with other business owners to strengthen and expand the way we do business and the services or products we deliver?

- Can I reorganize my business to allow myself to enjoy my life better?

Honest reflection, followed by a commitment to act, will perform miracles.

Time and time again business owners have done some soul searching and come up with some great ways to re-invent their business and give their clients the service they deserve!

The game of business is best played with enthusiasm and openness.
The top performing professional and/or successful business owner is one who is always 'on-the-grow', and on the look-out for ways to do it better. Are you? Invest a few minutes to jot down notes on how you might become that successful business or career champion.

Idea-rich Customer Service Tips

Don't just love them and leave them. After you've completed the sale, be available for the follow through. Make sure your in-house co-workers are aware of any special needs your client might have. Make sure you are accessible if your client has any questions. Follow up when appropriate to make sure things are going smoothly. Continue making your clients feel like they are the most important clients your firm has; often, based on referrals, they will be.

When I had my kitchen design studio, I would call clients a month or so after we had finished their new kitchen to schedule an installer visit. The installer would be told to adjust doors, hardware, drawers, and make any small repairs or tweaks on site. If something else was needed, he would let me know and we would order it and he would go back later to fix it. I told my installers, "They will tell you things they won't tell me, because I'm a nice guy. Get them to tell you and then you fix it. That way we both get more work and referrals down the road."

Take the extra time to go over the contract, specifications, finance arrangements, and delivery times to make sure you have covered your clients' needs. This is a good time to catch any mistakes, oversights, or *'I thought you said this was included?'* misunderstandings. Change it now and it's an adjustment. Change it later and it's an excuse or a mistake and stress.

Taking time to explain how something is manufactured will pay dividends. If your client understands the process and lead-times, they will be less likely to have unrealistic expectations or make demands you have trouble meeting. One of the owners of a cabinet manufacturer I had the privilege of working with would do that. Jack would give people a personal tour of the showroom and would take the time to explain how his cabinets were made (in detail including an industry 'best' warranty). I asked him why he did that when he had a good indication they were 'just' looking? **Jack Horner** told me, *"When I educate them on how better cabinets are made, they know what they are looking at when they shop elsewhere. And often they see the difference and come back to us."* Valuable lesson on customer service even if they don't become one right away.

"It is not enough to give the customer excellent service. You must subtly make him aware of the great service he is getting." Unknown, but wise writer

Finding your ideal client

Knowing who your target market 'really is' can be the secret to building a long-term profitable business. When you know who they are, it helps you understand their needs, what they want, and what goods and services you can profitably provide them.

As a business writer, facilitator, and keynote speaker, I am frequently asked about my market, my clientele, and my industry. I am fortunate that my creative approach works for professionals in many industries and that I can apply my *'Ideas At Work!'* to help them be more productive.

Who is your ideal client or customer? Who would you love to do business with on an ongoing basis? Who would you love to be working with now or in the long term?

Ask yourself:

Who is your ideal client/customer?

- Is it someone who can see the value in what you offer?
- Is it someone who has a demonstrated need for your service or products?
- Is it someone who is open to new ideas and processes in doing business?
- Is it someone who has the ability and the capacity to afford what you offer? Who can afford to buy what you sell?
- Is it someone who will purchase repeatedly from you?
- Is it someone who has a track record or history of working or dealing with someone like you or in using similar products or services?
- Is it someone who pays his or her bills on time and is a low maintenance or non-demanding customer?
- Is it someone who willingly refers you to other qualified prospects and becomes a champion or center of influence on your behalf?

Sounds like a dream client/customer, doesn't it? The reality, there are people out there who will match this or other criteria in your search to build your business success and career. The secret is setting some realistic criteria to help you recognize them or at least recognize those who don't match up.

Many business owners and sales staff neglect spending enough time in the pre-qualifying process. Taking time to ensure your prospect 'actually' qualifies can make your sales career more than successful – it can transform it into a superstar launching pad. We'll talk about that later in this success guide.

If you want to be productive, make a tremendously outrageous income, still have a life, and be able to enjoy the fruits of your labour – this might be a good exercise for you. Invest some time exploring who you would like to have as a long-term customer. Interestingly enough, this works very well. ☺

Visit: www.SuccessPublications.ca/BusinessSuccess-Tips.html for special business building success video tips, just for you.

Idea-rich Customer Service as a sales tool for higher prices

If you are looking for a way to differentiate yourself from your completion and minimize having to offer discounts, exceptional customer service works. More so if you happen to be a smaller company (or project that smaller, friendly image to your prospective clients). According to a 2011 **American Express** survey 80% of North Americans thought that smaller companies placed a greater emphasis on customer service. In that same survey respondents indicated (70%) they were willing to spend more with companies they believed provide excellent customer service. They also mentioned (59%) they'd try a new brand or company if it provided a better customer service experience.

Think about who you do business with now. For example, I drive out of my way to use a dry cleaner that treats me special. There are several other vendors that get my business because of their service. I don't mind the difference in price, because I know what I am getting, and I like it.

According to a Customer Experience Impact report by **Harris Interactive**, 90% indicated they would pay 'more' to ensure they got a superior customer service.

Unless you are a BIG-BOX type of operation, competing on price is not the most effective way to build or sustain your business. Exceptional service delivered each time is a great defense against even the toughest competition – customer service that provides what they really need, delivered with expertise and a great attitude. Make them feel special, treat them right, and they will come back to you and bring their friends. Discovered **Legacy Jewellers** in Fort Sask. who differentiate themselves by better service. Love their work!

Guess what?

There are people outside of North America... and they are checking you out!

With the advent and rapid expansion of global internet use, more companies are entering a new arena in marketing and customer service. Is there a fortune to be made for your company? Or is it a black hole to pour money into and hope someone out there is reading it? Worse yet, how are people who live in non-English speaking areas able to take advantage of your services?

Experts predicted Western European Internet users would match or surpass those in North America by the early part of this new century. With 50% of all Internet users estimated to live outside North America it would make sense to think seriously about how you serve such a diverse mixture of customers. Gee, 24-hour orders and on-line hits seven days a week. Sounds like a dream, or nightmare if you're not ready – doesn't it? Can they 'find' you when they are looking for help – either locally or from around the globe?

"Identifying a foreign market is only the first step," say experts. *"Actually tapping into it is a far trickier matter."* Looking at this emerging market from a North American viewpoint won't work to exploit this opportunity. Depending on your company you may need to set up and implement delivery and warehousing infrastructures with access and understanding of foreign currencies, laws, and business norms. You would need to translate and maintain content that presents or captures the various nuances, subtleties, and tastes of another culture, not your own.

This means getting to understand how the various nationalities you intend marketing to think and shop. Customer service just entered a challenging new era. One way would be to partner with local firms and strategic alliances in the major areas in which you feel you might draw new customers. **What if you want them to visit you here in_____?** Then what?

"European companies, in particular, have an advantage over US companies because they're used to dealing with different cultures and doing business multiple languages," according to **Forrester Research** director John C. McCarthy. *"We (North America) are used to living in a monolithic English cocoon."* The net may cross borders with ease, but capturing different cultures is more than just giving them 'access' to an English-speaking site.

There are some new Internet based startups that are responding to this new challenge. Some of these companies will help tackle the challenges of language and cultural issues in addition to translation services. Not cheap, but less expensive than blowing your first foreign impression. Expanding your company's presence on-line will be a challenge, but the effort will be worth it. Remember new customers require a new level in Customer Service.

> **According to Jim Jansen**, Pew Research Center's Internet and American Life Project, 58% of North Americans perform online research about the products and services that they are considering purchasing. The **Touch Agency** discovered Customers are 75% more likely to purchase from a brand they follow on Twitter. Engaging with your prospective and existing customers on-line is becoming a 'must do activity' if we are to remain competitive in this international business community. Hint: Where do your clients spend time on-line?

Idea-rich Customer Service – An international perspective

While reading *'Make ME Feel Special!'* ideas will pop into your mind that will help increase your business, expand your effectiveness, and increase your client satisfaction and referrals, ideas on how to re-position yourself as an expert in your area or field of business. Use the blank page at the back of the book to jot them down as they occur.

Principles made personal yield powerful results – Ideas At Work!

Someone once wrote, ***"There is nothing new under the sun".*** Although viewing the massive advertising and information we contend with daily, you'd wonder if that were true. There are, however, new twists and adaptations of basic ideas and formats that we use in 'innovative' ways to create new products, services, and information.

- **What hasn't changed** is our client's desires for value-added service.
- **What has changed** is the time demands on our clients and ourselves, the availability to communicate at the speed of thought and the demands on service that brings, and of course the increased mobility of our clients. They have many more choices globally now than at any time in our history. How do you help them chose to give their trust and business to you?

Our ability to help our clients is directly related to our willingness to put ourselves in their shoes and truly see things from their perspective.

This skill helps you get what you want – happy, SATISFIED clients who repeatedly send their friends back to see you to purchase products and services. Clients/customers who become your Fans and Champions!

The time we spend in understanding the real needs of our clients and why they buy is critical. **The time we spend training our staff to better serve our clients is one of the most cost-effective investments we can make in our success and long-term profitability.** The time we spend training our clients to help their customers is what will help us succeed as suppliers. It is part of what will set us apart from our competition and give us that edge in an increasingly competitive global market.

I believe true customer service is anticipating our client's needs and then positioning ourselves to meet or exceed them.

> **"Customer service isn't just 'a part' of your business.**
> **Customer service 'IS' your business!"**

A few years ago, I spoke for the Yukon tourism industry at the request of the Territorial Government. With major changes in the economic fabric of the Yukon, tourism is taking on an increased focus as a generator of goodwill, finance, and employment. More foreign tourists are being drawn to their area. They asked me back for a special presentation within a month for an international gathering on tourism in Whitehorse.

Perhaps you, too, cater to an international market. I find it a nice challenge and love the travel.

Understanding and adapting to meet their diverse needs, along with the North American customer mix already in place, is essential to your ability to grow and survive in an increasingly competitive global market.

- What changes have you made to your business to adapt to your wider range of clients?
- When will you make the changes necessary to survive and thrive?
- What training have you given your employees to help them succeed and represent you in a positive and helpful manner?
- What changes have you made in your perspective of service and business as it relates to international and divergent customers?

Master, who is my customer?

Many years ago, a young servant came to his wise and rich master and enquired of him how he should be successful in business.

The wise Master said, *"By taking care of the real needs and providing value for your customers."* The young servant replied, *"But Master, who is my customer?"*

This *plagiarized* parable from my Sunday school days illustrates the confusion we all too often have in business. **"Who is our client/customer?"** I would contend that we have both internal and external client/customers.

External customers are those who would do business with us and allow us to make a profit. Why would it be important to make sure we take care of the needs of our external customers?

Internal customers are those who assist us in making our business successful by playing a part (co-workers, staff) or supplying something we need to be successful. The same question on taking care of our internal customers' needs requires a bit more thought, doesn't it?

Why would it make sense to take care of those who work along-side you in your business or do part of the sales, delivery, or installation process?

For your client/customer, they are the company and each time they encounter one of them (touch point or moment of truth), your reputation and referral factor is on the line. Why would it make sense to take care of those who supply you with products or services? None of us work in isolation, do we?

In a pinch when you 'just gotta have it!' – who do you think your suppliers will help? Why? What can you do to build a relationship that returns that response?

What are you committed to doing to increase your effectiveness serving your external customers and internal customers alike? When will you implement it?

"Quality is never an accident. It is always the result of: High intention, Sincere efforts, Intelligent direction, and Skillful execution. It represents the wise choice of many alternatives."
Unknown

Idea-rich customer service redefined

"How can I reinvent myself or my company to better serve you and provide for your changing needs?"

Is there some service or other product I should be providing that would make 'your' experience easier, more rewarding, or user friendly? You need to ask yourself and your customers these types of questions on a frequent basis. Remember, if you aren't asking these questions — your competitors are!

Here are a few tools to use to help you keep and expand your market edge, tools to keep your clients/customers happy and coming back for more.

Customer surveys. Checking in on a regular basis to ask a few questions will work wonders. Look at the survey on page 93 for some tips to make this more effective.

Telephone polls. Sometimes a quick phone call to selected clients/customers will be enough to keep you informed and current as to how well you are doing. It's a great way to continue your conversation and help improve your relationship. How about actually calling a month or so after you've delivered your service or product to see how it is going and how the customers are enjoying it? Not too many businesses are doing this! Sad, as this is a business building success tool.

Service calls. These are often a neglected form of information as to the true satisfaction of your customers and the serviceability of your products. Make your service team part of your information gathering team and apply what you learn to make yourself better.

Focus groups. Take some time and invite a few of your 'best' customers to sit down and discuss honestly what you offer and what you deliver (from their experience). Put your ego on hold and listen carefully as they give you a very valuable gift — a gift that will help you succeed.

Product sampling. What a great way to find out what your customers want and what you can provide professionally and profitably. This allows you to test market and adjust before you go full tilt into a new product or service roll out. This might even be a perk for your 'best' clients who buy on a more frequent basis and might be the ones who refer you.

Web site or email feedback. This is emerging as a great way to allow your clients to tell you how you are doing, what they like, what they don't like and what they would like. It's a great way to share suggestions, changes and updates with your customers at their convenience. And often they will share ideas that will solve problems for each other as well.

8 Field-Proven Tips to Increase Your Income

Most of us in business (selling profession) are driven by goals. One goal is finding ways to increase our sales (income) and reduce our time demands in doing so. **Is this an achievable goal?** YES! One of the ways of doing that is in converting your 'one time' customers into regular buyers/clients who come back again and again to buy from you. Better yet, they bring their friends, too. This is one of the best ways of increasing your income.

Finding ways to get your potential and current customers to 'buy in larger quantities' is a valuable goal. Of course, finding new customers and getting qualified leads and referrals from existing customers is still a valid goal. **Here are some practical tips**, which when applied, allow you to hone your sales skills and accomplish these goals.

Become an Avid Reader (Leaders are readers!)

There are essentially only two ways to learn new things. One is through your own experience; the other, more effective way, is 'leveraged learning' through other people's experiences. Professionals are readers in search of new ideas, methods, and training materials to equip themselves to better prospect, qualify, sell, and then successfully build long-term customer relationships. What profitable ideas have you learned from someone else lately?

Have Fun Selling and Serving!

You spend more time working than any other activity in your life, so why not enjoy the time you invest in the selling/customer service process? Don't just think of selling as work. View it as enjoyable as any of your favorite family, leisure, or sports activities. When you get good at it – that's what happens anyway. People 'earn and learn' more in times of enjoyment!

Attend Training Seminars to Hone Your Selling/Service Skills

Don't wait on your company to lead or train you! Invest in yourself and your selling future. We can help!

There is no better way to learn a skill than attending a seminar or selling boot camp by street smart, successful sales experts. This is a true success secret from the business and selling superstars! Buy Secret Selling Tips.☺

Delegate Effectively

The majority of your selling/customer service time should be spent meeting with prospects and customers – not just doing administrative busy work! Follow-up and paperwork are a solid part of the selling/customer service process, but don't allow yourself to get bogged down in this area.

Subscribe to Informative Newsletters (read and apply)

Subscribe to successful 'selling' and motivational newsletters to keep up to date on hot new techniques and ideas for your business. There's nothing better than getting a regular helping of fresh hot new ideas and perspectives from experts on business or selling. Invest time to read, reflect, and ACT!

Have the Right Attitude about Selling, Service, and Business

The right attitude about selling, service, and business will carry you through, regardless of what challenges or obstacles are thrown in your way. Learning to view prospecting as natural and selling as an ongoing event, will make you a champion. It will also make you wealthy! Building solid relationships which generate repeat business begins with the right attitudes.

Don't Make Excuses for Your Lack of (Selling) Success

Under-performers love to have a scapegoat to blame for their failures or lack of achievement. If you talk to them, it is always something – the economy, the competition, the product, or the price… anything other than 'themselves' and their lack of commitment or performance. As a successful businessperson, you realize that your success, or lack of it, is totally, 100% your responsibility! Take personal leadership of your (selling/service) role and take corrective steps to add to your skills and succeed.

Welcome Your Mistakes as Learning Opportunities

Everyone makes mistakes. Successful professionals realize mistakes are a part of their learning curve and maximize the lesson from each one. *"Next time I will do _____ "* is their professional response to a new learning experience. Don't spend your time worrying or feeling victimized by mistakes. Instead spend 99% of your time thinking about a solution, as do the selling/service superstars! It works!

Confidence about Credibility

"No one gets taken seriously in this world unless he or she has credibility. Not credibility about brilliant ideas, or heroic deeds, but credibility about daily habits and performance."

There are four crucial Credibility Habits

Successful business is built on established credibility. Your customers want to be able to trust and rely on you to do what you say you'll do – when you say you'll do it. Here are the four ways in which we establish our credibility. How would you rate yourself and your co-workers or staff in these areas? Are there areas in which you see improvement needed?

Showing up on time

Time is the most valuable commodity we have. It is precious in that it is finite and cannot be banked or saved – it must be used wisely. When you devalue my time – you devalue me! Show me that I can count on you to be there when you say you will, and I will begin to trust you.

Doing what you say

Following through and doing what you say is very rare. We expect to be disillusioned, to be lied to, and to be disappointed. When we aren't, we are pleasantly surprised and your credibility soars with us. **Under promise and over deliver!**

Finishing what you start

What a nice surprise, when we discover that you finish what you start. What a difference this makes in the corporate field. Doing this will set you apart from your competition. Resolve to start and complete what you commit to doing if you would build a successful business or career.

Saying please and thank you

Common courtesy is not that common. As individuals, we are too often treated with a lack of civility or respect. Show appreciation for people and their willingness to pursue dealing with you or buying from your firm. This will serve you well and help win my loyalty as a client.

These simple habits may seem self-evident, but the failure to observe them is probably the biggest cause of loss of credibility in business.

In an increasingly competitive global economy, our customers want to feel special, and they want to be able to trust you. How would you rate yourself and your company in this area? How would you change what you're doing now to ensure they get that opportunity?

The Secret of the Seed!

I travel a bit. When home, I used to have coffee with my old buddy Steve (my, then, 94-year-old neighbor) and his two *'younger'* farmer friends (Mike, 80 and Peter, 78 respectively). Over the few years I learned a lot about farming that is directly applicable to what we do in life, sales, and in business. I've grown to appreciate the effort and challenges our farmers go through to help feed us. They are amazing, hardworking, and productive people. Sadly, they are gone. Now nephews Mickey and Scott have taken on the farming.

Mike and Peter rotated their crops based on their 'best guess' at what would be the best offering in the market for the coming year. They planted canola, wheat, barley, or peas, as selected, each year. When they planted wheat in the spring, they expected to harvest wheat that fall. There is an *'expectation'* that the seeds they planted would produce the crops they expected. They would be very surprised to plant canola and get barley, for example. **This is the secret of the seed!**

Interestingly enough, I see people planting seeds for failure and then expecting successful or different results in their sales, business, or life. They are surprised when things fail or don't work to their misguided expectations. **Here is the secret of the seed: you get what you plant, nurture, and harvest. Exceptional customer service follows this principle.**

- **Plant the seeds** of creative, personal leadership and responsibility,
- **Plant the seeds** of continuous encouragement, to dream and stretch,
- **Plant the seeds** of equipping your team with the tools and the motivation to win,
- **Plant the seeds** of personal discipline and long-term focus,
- **Plant the seeds** of co-operative innovation and competition,
- **Plant the seeds** of high standards and personal excellence in customer service,
- **Plant the seeds** of creating value-added products and superior services we (*customers*) *actually* need,

...and **harvest** abundance and success at the end of your labours.

What makes 'YOU-nique?'

"To my customer,
I may not have the answer, but I'll find it.
I may not have the time, but I'll make it.
I may not be the biggest,
but I'll be the most committed to your success!"
Anon

In a world of increasing 'me-too's' and 'sorta-like's' and 'ditto's' what makes you stand out from the crowd? What **'YOU-niqueness'** do you bring to the marketplace that will make your potential customers want to deal with you and return time and time again? Are there things you do that your customers aren't expecting?

Take a few minutes and give some creative thought to these questions. Analyze your answers, for in them are revealed the secrets of your eventual success and competitive edge.

- What do I provide my customers that **they can't get everywhere else**?
- What can I do to follow-up as a thank you to people – even those who don't buy from me now?
- What can I say or give to my customers that will influence them to remember me and the experience they enjoyed with my firm?
- What 'extra-unexpected-value' can I provide my customers after they buy from me?
- What can I give my customers that will totally amaze them – something they would never expect?
- How can I build long term relationships and communicate with clients/customers and their families that will influence them to remember me for years to come?

Based on careful thought – what changes will you commit yourself to making which will ensure these 'You-nique' factors become part of your daily operation? When will you start?

"Smart businesses should come to realize that the customer service bar is lower — and that today, it's easier than ever to differentiate your company from the pack with (crazy as it seems) actual quality customer service."
Brad Tuttle, *"A Few Thoughts on the God-Awful State of Customer Service"*, Time, 2010.

Understanding why people buy... and how I can re-position myself to take advantage of that reasoning

People make purchases, accept offers, or decide to frequent a specific store or vendor for a variety of reasons. They buy into benefits. The better you understand the reasons they buy, as related to your product or service, the better you will be equipped to convince them to buy from you. Your research and conversations with them can uncover the keys to gaining and retaining them as customers. *'Idea-rich customer service'* is offering me what I really need, not just what you sell or what I ask for!

The following benefits reflect the reasons people buy in order of importance. Remember each prospect is different, as is each product or service. Your product or service might not offer all these benefits. That might be ok, or maybe not – you decide! However, is there some way to modify or position your product or service to offer each benefit?

Unleash your Business Potential **- offer customers more reasons to deal with you! Here are ten reasons why people make decisions to buy or engage the services of a professional or business.**

1. **To make money/acquire or possess**
Describe how your product or service offers me the potential for profit or a potential gain.

2. **To save money or prevent future loss**
Describe how your product/service offers ways to save me money.

3. **To save time**
Describe how your product/service can save me time.

4. **For recognition**
Describe how your product/service offers me recognition or status.

5. **For security/peace of mind**
Describe how your product/service offers me security or peace of mind.

6. **For convenience/comfort**
In what ways does your product/service provide for my convenience or comfort?

7. **For flexibility**
How does your product/service rate in flexibility? In what areas? How?

8. **For satisfaction/reliability/pleasure or entertainment**
How does your product/service stack up in these areas? Why is that important to me?

9. **For status or pride of ownership/ gratify ego or impress others**
How does your product/service add to my status or pride of ownership?

10. **For health reasons**
Is there some way that your product/service will contribute to my health?

Drop me an email and I'll send you the full list of **50 emotional reasons why people buy.** bob@ideaman.net

Understanding the answers to these questions will give you an edge in gaining, serving, and keeping your customers. Being able to present your product or service from the perspective of meeting your client's needs, by appealing to their desired benefits, can be critical to your success.

The more you know about your client, your product/service, and your competition, the better equipped you are to effectively do business. Can you think of any other reasons why people would want to do business with you?

What's YOUR U.S.P.?

Following our 'What makes You-nique' section we thought it might be valuable for you to sit down with your team or staff and think about what your Unique Selling/Service Proposition really is. What advantage do you have or need to separate yourself from your competitors locally and globally?

Seriously consider each of these typical USPs. Some might be applicable; many will simply be an 'ME too' response. It's not unique if everyone does it or can offer it. Be willing to dig deep and prove your points here.

- **Selection**
- **Big or volume discounts**
- **Advice or assistance**
- **Top of the line (high end)**
- **Speedy service**
- **Service beyond the basics**
- **Convenience**
- **Better warranty/guarantee (compared to whom?)**

Killing the 'termites' of BAD or ineffective service

I had a friend who bought a lovely wood frame cabin in a picturesque spot in BC's interior. He really enjoyed owning this place and looked forward to escaping the pressures of his hectic career to relax there.

This changed one year when it was discovered that he had a nest of 'termites' in one area of his wooden foundation. Now fortunately for him, they were discovered and 'eradicated' in time, before he would have had to replace the whole foundation. Termites eat holes or tunnels through the wood to get where they want to go and, in the process, seriously undermine the structural integrity. In time the structure collapses when the foundation can no longer support the weight of the building. You can't see it from the outside. It takes careful and regular inspections to ensure that termites aren't eating away.

I thought about that in relation to our careers and businesses. In many instances a once brilliant career stalls and the person is relegated to the 'also rans. All too often a business 'folds' and people wonder 'Why?'. (Well, not the dissatisfied customers!) In many cases, the 'termites' of BAD or ineffective service have done their secret work in weakening the structure until it finally collapsed. Covid simply accelerated this process for many businesses.

But it doesn't have to happen. Regular check-ups will make sure your Customer Service isn't infested with 'termites'. It is possible to ensure they don't get in, by having a solid training foundation and encouraging an ongoing value-based service culture. It takes diligence, constant commitment, and leadership-by-example from the owner or manager, but it can be done.

I'd suggest a little check-up *'from the neck up'*, might be a good place to start.

- **Values**
- **Motives**
- **Attitude**

Let's talk about Values. They drive our attitudes and motives and the way we behave in public. Values are an inner guidebook, if you will, that direct or influence our behavior. They are the 'unwritten rules' by which we live our lives – and they show up in everything we do. Whether we like to admit it or not – our behavior is very often consistent with our values. Let me ask you another question: What are the 2 or 3 most important values in your life? Take a moment and seriously consider this question.

Now, the real question. How are these 'values' showing up in your career, business, or dealings with your clients? How can you better focus these values to help you provide real value-based customer service?

Motives reflect the reasons 'WHY' I do what I do. For example, you may work hard and diligently to be noticed or gain a competitive edge in business. You may also work hard because it's expected. Or you may work hard because you believe in giving 100% in everything you do. Take a moment and ask yourself 'WHY' you do some of the things you do on the job. Are there areas that might use a tune up?

Attitudes reflect the way we think. They reflect in the way we work and show to the world what we really value. They really show up in how we relate to people. Hint: it can't be faked! If your customers are a source of interruption and grief for you – it shows! If they are a welcome addition to your day – it shows!

- What do your actions say about your attitudes?
- Did you recognize a few attitudes that needed a spring-cleaning?
- What changes are you committed to making in your attitudes?

Doing some research will give you a good idea where you may have areas of concern or 'termites' working deep inside your business or actions of your personnel. One way of doing that would be to conduct 'exit' interviews (or hire someone to do them) as customers leave your place of business.

Think about the last time you shopped somewhere or were dealing with a business. Ask yourself some of these questions. Then, look at your business and ask the same ones or have them asked. The answers might surprise you!

1. When I entered the store, how well was I greeted and made to feel comfortable?
2. While I was in the store, how did they make me feel important?
3. During my shopping or business experience, did they effectively find out what I wanted or needed? Did they help me get what I wanted?
4. In my conversations with staff, how effectively was I listened to?
5. As I left, what did they do that would encourage me to want to come back again?

Visit: www.SuccessPublications.ca/BusinessSuccess-Tips.html for special business building success video tips, just for you.

Let me ask you a series of pertinent questions about your career or business.

1. After having contact with you – how would you like people to **feel**?
2. What would you want them to **say** about you?
3. Would you want them to **tell** their friends about their experience with you?

As mentioned previously, do you have a current and *relevant* MISSION STATEMENT?

- Is it something that all your team/staff have had input in developing and agree with its aims?
- Is it clear and concise to make it easy to remember?
- Is it visible for customers and staff alike to see while in the work environment? If not, WHY NOT?

Remember it needs to be a 'living' document. By that I mean on a regular basis it should be dusted off, revisited, and revamped to ensure it is current and relates to your changing customer and staff expectations.

EXIT Statements or interviews

> **Exercise**: Take a moment and write your own exit statement. Visualize an impartial person stationed outside your place of business, who is primed to ask each person who leaves the following question: **"How would you describe the experience and treatment you've just had in _____?"**

If someone were to ask that question to each of your clients/customers, what would you want their response to sound like? Take a moment and write down your best-desired response.

Now, if this is the response you'd like to hear, and you see a GAP between that and what they most likely receive now – what needs to change?

If you really want people to say what you desire about you and your business, what needs to change in these areas? This is where you build a foundation that is resistant to 'termites' and will support a successful career and business.

What changes are you committed to making personally and corporately in each of the following areas?

Attitudes

Motives

Values

Greetings

Answering questions and finding solutions

Being a resource center

Staff training

Management training

Personal training

Policy flexibility training

Mission statement update

Technology updates and training for effective use

Physical layout and structure

Selection and placement of goods

Services offered

When you build a concrete foundation under your commitment to 'value-added' customer service-based business you begin to build a business that will thrive and grow.

- When will you start?
- What obstacles stand in your way?
- How will you overcome them?

Visit: www.SuccessPublications.ca/FeelSpecial.htm for special bonus resources, just for our readers.

Because the Customer

Because the customer has a need,
We have a job to do.

Because the customer has a choice,
We must be the better choice.

Because the customer has sensibilities,
We must be considerate.

Because the customer has an urgency,
We must be quick.

Because the customer is unique,
We must be flexible.

Because the customer has high expectations,
We must excel.

Because the customer has influence,
We have the hope of more customers.

Because of the customer,
We exist.

Author Unknown

Focusing on my clients helps brings clarity to what I offer them. It allows me to invest in areas which profitably serve their needs while helping me build and expand my business. This same focus allowed me to relax while speaking as I learned it wasn't about me – it was about them!

The Seven Be-Attitudes of Great Service

Customer Service is one of the foundations for any enduring business success. It does depend on more than just a catchy slogan to engage the minds and hearts of everyone on your team. It takes leadership and ongoing commitment on the part of owners and managers to show, employees and clients alike, the true essence of Customer Service.

"Customer Service is not just 'a part' of your business. Customer service 'is' your business!"

A few guiding principles might be helpful. Here are 7 'Be-Attitudes,' I trust will be of assistance in sharing the importance of customer service all year. I've been sharing them around the globe for the past 15 plus years.

1. **Be professional** – put the customer first. Present yourself and your company in a professional manner. A professional is always looking for ways to help the client and to make their life better by offering products or services that work for them.

2. **Be polite** – wouldn't you expect to be given consideration and respect? Remember to give your clients the same courtesy, regardless of the kind of day you may be having.

3. **Be prompt** – do your best to not keep customers waiting. If you promise something, do everything you can to deliver on time; or call and let the customer know exactly what time to expect you. Try not to keep a customer waiting on the phone or in your store either.

4. **Be proud** – you are an expert, a solutions provider to your clients. Be proud of your expertise and ability to help your customers.

5. **Be personal** – remember your customers are individuals. Don't you hate it when people treat you like just another number? Make a commitment to treat every customer as an individual - it will make him or her feel special, because they are!

6. **Be persistent** – good service isn't always given on the first encounter. Be persistent in your efforts to serve and solve their problems. If your customer has a problem with your service or product, persistence in making sure they are satisfied, or the problem is rectified to their needs is essential.

7. **Be patient** – some customers need a little more time or assistance to make their selection. Taking the time, especially with our seniors or children, is the true sign of a customer service professional.

These *7 'Be-Attitudes' of customer service* will not guarantee you success in business. They will, however, give you one of the foundations for success in building a business that will still be here well into the next 'decade or three' to serve your clientele actively and profitably.

They will also give you a guideline to lead by example and to train those to whom you entrust your business and your reputation – your staff!

Little hinges swing big doors

While travelling North America and more recently the globe I share a few basic ideas or messages with my audiences. I tell them, **"Once people fully understand the 'Why?' (purpose) the 'How's?' (processes or procedures) tend to take care of themselves."** Simple little idea, isn't it? However, these little things seem to slip the grasp of many North American leaders. We tend to complicate things.

W. Clement Stone, who built a billion dollar 'sales' organization out of the depths of the great depression (*early 1900's*), shared an *idea-rich, key* quote that has been close to my own growth and success. He worked with Napoleon Hill, who authored, *'Think and Grow Rich'*, co-published *'Success Magazine'*, and later mentored Og Mandino, who authored motivational classic, *'The Greatest Salesman in the World'*.

Stone wrote: ***"Little hinges swing big doors."***

Successful, entrepreneurial leaders constantly search and are open to finding the next 'slight edge', the next profitable idea, or 'little hinge'. I do too! Building a client focused culture can be one of those little hinges.

"It's the little things that make the big things possible. Only close attention to the fine details of any operation makes the operation first class," offered J. Willard Marriott.

What 'little things' can you add to your mix to make a difference?

Friendly works!

"A customer is the most important visitor on our premises. The customer is not dependent on us – we are dependent on him or her." Anonymous

I was reminded of these sage words as we relaxed and reflected in a quaint little hotel and spa in Puerto Vallarta, Mexico. I'm sure; they could have easily been penned by many Mexican businesspeople, as this attitude was very evident by my hosts.

I am consistently amazed at the open friendliness and genuine attitude of customer service so evident everywhere I travel down here. Our hosts and staff seem genuinely glad to see us when we come to eat, get a towel for the beach or pool, ask for a cab to the marina, or ask directions to the local market. (We found similar attitudes on our trips to Cuba.)

You'd never know that, on average, they make only about $8-$12 for a hard day's work. It can't be only for the tips, as they are included in the all-inclusive package I booked. What is it that drives them to be so hospitable while working so hard? You'd never know it from their happy demeanor, even toward the end of a long day working diligently to serve their customers. Their smiles are like a handshake from a close friend. They make you feel welcome.

We went for a sail on the **Pacific Dreams Gypsy Spirit**, *a 60-foot ketch rigged ship with a crew of three and a couple of helpers from adjacent boats. Our host and his crew were very gracious to our needs and even let me take the wheel for most of the trip across the bay to the private little beach at a small fishing village. Our host took us snorkeling, pointing out the various fish and underwater sites, while the crew prepared an amazing lunch on a beach side grill – way beyond what I would have expected for the price of the trip. Again, a genuine interest in me and in making sure we all had a great sail.*

- When was the last time you walked into a store or place of business and had some one look up and see a genuine smile of joy and acceptance cross their face?
- When did you welcome a customer or colleague in this manner?
- What needs to change to instill this level of interaction and service?

Perhaps we can each learn a lesson from my Mexican friends in how to enhance our customers experience with us. Do you think that might help you build your career or business?

Are you 'here' to serve me?

Picture this: Have you ever walked into a retail store and stood there looking, in vain, for someone to help you?

Have you ever seen groups of employees (*I wouldn't call them professional salespeople*) standing together, talking, and tried to catch their attention? Or watch as one of them reluctantly tears themselves away and walks over to ask you, *"What you want?"* They might even be 'programmed' to say, *"May I help you?"* Can you picture that in your mind?

Let's take a different snapshot. Have you ever been in a store and been 'pounced' on by an over-eager salesperson who obviously wants to 'sell you' something? Ever defended yourself with, *"No thanks, just looking!"* even though you had come in with a specific purchase in mind? I have, all too often.

How did you feel in either of these situations? Did you feel special?

My guess – not so special, right? What went through your mind at the time? Well, that is what your potential customers have in the back of their minds when they walk into your store, or when you walk into their office. People are a bit nervous when dealing with salespeople... they are afraid we are going to 'sell' them something. Interestingly enough, people love to buy; they just don't like being sold.

In our on-line *'Secret Selling Tips'* series we talked about the importance of setting goals, and we challenged our readers to **"Set a goal so big, that if you achieved it, it would blow your mind."**

For you to make that BIG, 'Visionary' goal a reality you need to interact more 'effectively' with your potential customers. Whether you are prospecting, making sales calls, or working in a retail environment, understanding, and applying the 'foundations to success' in customer service and selling are important.

Sales/Service 101: Greet your customers with enthusiasm

At its most basic level, the opening or greeting is an initial step or foundation to establish connection and build trust with a potential client. These 'windows of attention', where you have the opportunity to start and build a connection, are typically short.

It has been repeatedly proven that people do 'more' business with those they like and trust.

Whether you work in a retail environment, make client calls, or provide a professional service, how you make them 'feel' is important to your long-term profitability and business.

70% of buying experiences are based on how the customer 'feels' they are being treated, according to a study by **McKinsey & Company**.

As a business owner or manager, professional service provider, or selling professional, a crucial part of your role is to create that environment where your potential client/customer feels comfortable and open to working with or buying from you, an environment where they feel you are there to help them. This can be in a retail setting, on the phone, on the web, or when you make an on-site visit. This is not the 'qualifying stage' where you find out specifics or probe their needs, simply your opening or introducing yourself and your company in 'conversational' dialogue. This is simply the beginning of your sales, business engagement conversation with them.

Keep your opening objective in mind. Create immediate interest for additional discussion and engage or connect with the prospect or customer. That means asking open ended questions that encourage your potential customers to talk.

For example:

"Good morning, my name is Bob... What brings you into our store today?"
Or *"Have you seen our special offers on _____?"*
Much more engaging than *"May or Can I help you?"*

The first two 'open-ended' questions might get you an informative answer which can begin a productive dialogue. The 3rd one might get you, "No, thanks... just looking!" Some sales leaders suggest making personal comments about the weather or *"How was the drive to our store?"* What works for you?

We suggest working on this 'key' selling/customer service skill until you have a collection of genuine openings that you are fully comfortable using, openings that reflect who you 'are' and not just the same ones your fellow sales members use. Keep in mind, if it is too routine, it will sound routine. Also, keep in mind, customers will hear what your team members use. That can diminish the work you have already done when they recognize a 'canned' opening. How do you react to a slick, canned, sales pitch?

Motivation: Remember your role as a professional is to 'help' your clients/customers find what they need at a price they can afford. **Make it 'easy' for them to do business with you.**

Whichever you approach you use, make sure you ask from the perspective of someone who is 'genuinely' interested in 'them' and smile. Make sure your body language reinforces you are 'actually' glad to see them.

Never underestimate the power of a 'genuine' smile as a foundation for success in the selling/customer service game. Make them feel welcome and not an interruption in your day, and you are on the path to sales success. If you are working in a retail environment, make sure a new customer knows you 'see' them enter your store. Perhaps, you can make eye contact, wave, and smile.

Give them a few seconds to orient themselves and 'settle in' before you walk over, so they don't feel rushed or pounced on. As a professional, I would always introduce myself to potential clients.

If you do get something like, "*Just looking or just getting ideas,*" don't take it as a rejection, simply a reflection that your customer is not ready to open up to you yet. Sometimes they are just looking or doing research. Use this as an opportunity to direct them to an area where you have a product or service that might assist them in their exploration. Perhaps you can say, "*We have some amazing products or services. If I knew what you were considering, I would be happy to direct you to that area.*"

You can also use this as an opportunity to set up a 'check back' with them. Suppose they really are just looking. Your response might be something like, "*I'm sure you'll find some fantastic items in our store. We are quite proud of what we offer. May I check back with you to see if you have any questions?*" Perhaps, just say, *"I'll check back with you to see if you have any questions, or I can be of any assistance."* Smile, pause, and walk away. Don't hover!

Make sure they know you are there to help, but they do not feel pressured with you hovering over their shoulders. This sets the foundation for further dialogue on the road to a successful sale.

Visit: www.SuccessPublications.ca/BusinessSuccess-Tips.html for special business building success tips, just for you.

Asking Great Questions to Qualify Customers

"You've got to ask great questions to qualify your prospects and ask for the order. Otherwise, you're wasting your time." **Jeff Mayer**

Wisdom and experience, gleaned from generations of top performing sales leaders, business owners, and professional service providers teaches us that when you're able to ask 'better' questions you can do a much 'better' job of qualifying and helping your prospects become long-term customers.

The professional who invests the time to 'quickly' qualify their potential customers is the one who will have the best closing ratios and make more money by working with more qualified customers.

The professional who, when talking to a qualified customer, digs deep to discover their 'real' needs and wants will be the sales leader in any organization. Very much like the doctor who asks, *"Where does it hurt?"*

"Spend lots of time talking to customers face to face. You'd be amazed how many companies don't listen to their customers." **Ross Perot**

Sales/Service 101: The discovery process or how to pre-qualify a potential client/customer

The secret to becoming a H-U-G-E success in business (in any industry) is to have a comfortable, proven process to qualify potential clients/customers as a part of the selling process, a systematic, step-by-step process that you follow day-in and day-out. Create and refine your qualifying as part of the selling/customer service processes and it's easy to increase your revenues and profits without working more hours.

The discovery process is critical in the business arena. If you are working in a retail environment, more so one where advertising drives the sales process, a quick way to qualify will save you time and make you more money. Isn't that a better use of your time? Wouldn't you say, similar when making sales calls? **For example,** a couple visiting a furniture or appliance store to purchase a new fridge.

> You might ask questions that draw out what the customer is considering and what features, benefits, and price point would influence their decision to buy.

Ask about the old appliances as well as new purchase. For example:
- "What are the 3 things you would like in a new _____?"
- "What were the 3 things you didn't like about your old ____?"
- "What features did you have in mind for your new _____?"

Questions that help narrow the focus to specific choices. For example:
- "What color scheme did you have in mind?"
- "Does this piece have a specific color or pattern you like?"

Questions that lead to writing up an order. For example:
- "When would you like to have that delivered?"
- "Would you like to have us install it?"

Quick note: If your prospect's answers don't quite measure up to what you think they should be or don't tell you what you need – and you've made sure you've asked good questions, then in reality, you don't have a good prospect. Or, at least not at the present time. On the other hand, when the questions do measure up and you've discovered a problem you can solve, you've created a good sales opportunity for yourself.

Remember to summarize what you've learned in this discovery process before you move to the next action step in solving their problem or showing them something that fits their expressed needs.

Inevitably in any conversation things will slip through the cracks or misunderstandings will occur. This is your chance to allow the customer to correct them before you move into either creating a proposal, demonstration, or showing them samples for consideration.

Asking something like:

- *"Is that a fair summary of our discussions?"*
- *"Let me see if I have this correct? What you are looking for is_____."*
- *"Am I correct in my understanding?"*

What questions should you ask to better qualify your prospects? Create a list of 10 questions you can use in your specific situation that will draw out the information you need to qualify and then help your prospect.

Refine them, revamp them, revise them, and replace them until you have questions that are thoughtful, insightful, and emotionally engaging.

Discuss these with your fellow professionals. Asking questions your competition doesn't ask is a great way to not only differentiate yourself but reinforce your customer's confidence in your abilities and expertise to take care of them.

> *"To understand others, you should get behind their eyes and walk down their spines."* **Rod McKuen**

More Idea-rich Customer Service examples

Here's a quick tip ... if you want to take your customer service to the next level, you can start by just changing a few words. Instead of saying *"You're welcome,"* simply say *"It was my pleasure"*. It's a gracious response that is above and beyond normal speech. Four simple words that will propel you above and beyond average service as it will set you apart from everyone else!

Customer service is all about speaking in a language that everyone understands, while being warm, friendly, and approachable. People might not remember what you said, but they will never ever forget how you made them FEEL. That's customer service.

© *Katharine C. Giovanni, CCS www.KatharineGiovanni.com*

Take my truck

I was picking up an order of books, two thousand, in my VW. To say it was a load was a bit of understatement and I fully expected to make a few trips. When I pulled up to the loading dock at Friesens with my Jetta, the fellow on the dock asked if I really expected to pick up two pallets of books.

I explained that I lived in town and would make several trips to my garage, unload and be back. He reached into his pocket, pulled out his keys, and handed them to me, "My pickup is the blue Dodge in the parking lot; go get it and back it in here. When you're done put, it back in my parking place."

That's customer service, and not because of the company policy. This was the individual believing in the company.

© *Les Kletke www. globalghostwriter.com*

Qualifying 'continued' as a crucial step in your success

Your success in business can 'hinge' on how well you know your competition, your client/customer, and your capacity to provide solutions that capture their confidence and their business.

As mentioned earlier, sales are frequently lost when getting to know the client/customer, their needs, and wants is rushed or ignored in your haste to capture the sale. The secret to becoming successful in selling/customer service is to have a comfortable, proven process. Create and refine your qualifying as a key part of your selling success process and it's easy to increase your revenues and profits without working more hours.

Investing time to dig deeper as part of the client service/selling process achieves two essential things:

- It improves your chance of getting the eventual order or sale by building solid foundations to reveal and help solve your customer's problems.
- It sets the stage for a long-term mutually beneficial relationship as well as enhanced customer referrals and repeat business.

> *"Make your products easier to buy than your competition or you will find your customers buying from them."* Mark Cuban

You might want to know:

- **What is the client/customer's problem or opportunity you can solve?** You and the customer are talking about something. He or she is visiting your store or asking you to put a proposal together for some specific reason. What is the problem or opportunity? If there's no problem (challenge, opportunity, supply need, i.e., product or service under consideration), there's likely no sale.
- **What is the financial impact of the customer's problem?** How is the problem impacting them? Is there a way to 'quantify' the dollar amount or value of the problem? It must either be costing him money, wasting his time, or is just inconvenient. Perhaps it is a choice to improve or beautify a living space? How will it fit, how will it look, how will it feel? When you're able to get the customer to tell you how this is impacting their situation, your probability of closing the sale dramatically increases.
- **Who is the decision maker?** Are you talking with the decision maker? If not, it's often a complete and total waste of your time! In retail, who is your customer? When making sales calls this is even more important.

- **What is the decision-making process?** You need to know how your customer will decide to hire, engage your services, or buy from you. It's always enlightening when you ask, *"What criteria will you use to make your decision?"* Nice to know if they are openly shopping your competition, too. More often than not, the customer doesn't have a clue or is able to articulate it. Their answer enables you to ask more questions as you identify and define what is 'really' important to the customer.
- **Where is the sense of urgency?** If there's no sense of urgency nothing's going to happen! Why do they need to buy something? Why do they need to do it now? If you know the answer, you've probably got yourself a sale. If you don't, nothing's going to happen. Is it an advertised sales item or limited time offering?
- **Ask for the sale!** It's OK to ask for the sale at any stage in the selling /customer service process. In fact, that is your job! Using a soft or trial close is a great qualifying tool to check in with your customer. Plus, it can be fun to see what happens when you say something like this,
    - *"When do you want this _____ delivered?"*
    - *"Would you like to sign this agreement [contract, purchase order]?"*
    - *"Please sign or initial here."*

Your customer's reaction will tell you a lot about where the sales conversation and your selling/customer service opportunity is really going.

Remember, manage your probe time. Discuss and explore your potential customers' business facts or potential choices: timing, objectives, specifications, etc. quickly. Invest more of your time – 75 to 80% discussing 'their' problems or challenges in reaching 'their' goals, how these problems impact 'them', the cost of doing nothing, the rewards of acting, or resolving 'their' issues, and the options 'they've' considered so far. Don't skimp in establishing a relationship or your understanding of their needs, criteria, decision process, or ability to act.

One last hint: Don't be afraid to invest time to educate your potential client/customers on why you provide demonstrably better services, products, or how they work. That too is part of the qualifying process and a great way to demonstrate your expertise and professionalism as well. It builds relationships and repeat business as well.

> *"Do not follow where the path my lead.*
> *Go instead where there is no path and leave a trail."*
> **George Bernard Shaw**

Exploring solutions or Show and Sell

"Advice is like snow; the softer it falls, the longer it dwells upon, and the deeper it sinks into the mind." Samuel Taylor Coleridge

Ander and Stern who wrote **'Winning At Retail'** defined service from a customer's perspective: (1) knowing what I want and having it in stock; (2) helping me find the product I'm looking for easily without wasting my time; (3) providing information to answer my questions and assist me in making an intelligent choice with signs, brochures, a salesperson, via the internet; and, after you've done the first three right, (4) friendly, knowledgeable staff.

Sales/Service 101: Exploring or presenting solutions

The secret to increasing your conversion and closing ratios is simple: See the process through the eyes of your client/customer. Help them make the right 'buying' decision.

This step will challenge you to do your homework. You need to become and remain a 'knowledgeable' expert on your product and services to fully advise and assist your customer in making the right 'buying' decision. Remember, your customer may have done their homework on the web before they came in to see you. They will know when you are bluffing and your credibility as well as your sales will suffer. In fact, knowing your products and services will help you ask more intelligent, differentiating questions in the qualifying stage of the selling process.

"Purpose is the engine, the power that drives and directs our lives." John Noe

We wanted to give you a *quick* overview of this critical step in the customer service/selling process. Professionals make a sale when they show or demonstrate the value and personalize or translate those features to their customers. The top performers and leading business owners are often the most knowledgeable as well. If you have qualified well, you will already know which features to focus on and can move ahead to demonstrate their benefits and advantages to your customer.

Key to Remember: It is not the features that sell your product or service – it is those 'perceived' benefits or advantages those features 'bring' to your customers. Thinking about and sharing from the benefit/advantage point of view of your customer is the secret to your long-term success in business. It is also the secret to gaining referrals and repeat business.

Simple selling formula: create a series of **'so that'** statements to help your customer.

This [**Product/Service**] has [**feature**] which means [**benefit**] 'so that' you [**advantage**].

Once you've gone through the qualifying process with your potential customer you can confidently move into the **Show and Sell** (exploring solutions) stage in helping them select the right product or service for their specific needs.

A few suggestions to help you successfully navigate this stage.

- **Don't overwhelm them with choices or options.** For example: if they are shopping for a TV don't show them a TV Wall.
- Take them directly to the appropriate department or display area.
- **One secret gleaned from top selling professionals** is to give them a choice of 3 and show them the higher/best quality or higher priced selection first. Why, you ask? People like to be in control of their choices and not overwhelmed. Giving them a choice of 3 narrows it down and allows them to 'choose' or buy. Another factor, people will often surprise you and actually buy the higher quality or priced choices.
- **Demonstrate: This entails involving them and the rest of their 'buying' party** (who can have a direct influence on the decision). Get them to play with the buttons, open the drawers, change the channels in the home theatre room, lie down on a mattress, or sit on the sofa or recliner. Get them involved, let them touch it and enjoy it. Let them experience, if only for a moment, how it would feel to own and use that specific product. This is a great way to differentiate the various features between your three choices which also help in the final decision.
- **Hint:** Be ready to express and demonstrate those features, benefits, and advantages that most meet their expressed and un-expressed needs. However, be careful sharing your opinion. Your role as their own 'knowledgeable' advisor is that of a resource guide helping them make the right 'buying' decision for them.

This is a great opportunity to plant the seeds for an expanded sale and ongoing relationship. As you learn more about your customer you can 'logically' introduce additional components for their benefit into the mix. For example: accessories, additional pieces (e.g. TV Stand), special packages or pricing (e.g. Sofa, loveseat or chair; fabric protection), payment plans, protection or warranty programs which will complement their main purchase. **Challenge:** How well do you know the features, benefits, and advantages of your products and services?

- Invest time to break down and determine the more customer important features for your products and services.
- Make sure you know what benefits (to customer) each of those provide.
- Follow through to determine the advantage (to customer) for each benefit.

This is where you can access your training as well as ask your senior professionals for a little help. Preparing to meet the needs of your customers is an important part of the secret to success in selling.

Sales/Service 101: Reinforce good decisions and future

Another secret of leading professionals is based on considering the total lifetime value of your customer. Clients/customers can, if serviced well, become long time customers, and create repeat business as well as become a great source for referrals. That part of the business success process begins here, at the close of the initial purchase.

What must happen before the customer gets to enjoy the purchase they made from you?

- Does it need to be ordered, built, delivered, set up, or serviced?
- What is involved in that process that your customer needs to know now?

Taking a minute or two to go over their purchase and what needs to happen is a good investment of their time… it is imperative from your perspective. Doing this reduces the chance they will get home and go through what we call, 'buyer's remorse'. We all go through it at times.

Your role as their 'knowledgeable' advisor is to guide them in this process and to support their decision. That can be as simple as your honest observation, *"John, Pat… You've made a wise investment in this setting or this TV. I'm sure you'll enjoy it for years to come. Thank you for shopping here, we appreciate your business."* Or, if non-retail business, *"Thanks for your order; I'm sure it will serve you well."*

A simple thank you can work wonders in reinforcing your relationship and the good decision they made to deal with you. This is very much a personal decision, and you are part of the consideration too. Your last 60 seconds with your client can be the most important investment in your long term, mutually profitable relationship. Invest them well.

Remember: Customers for life is a worthy goal for the professional.

"Desire is the key to motivation, but it's the determination and commitment to an unrelenting pursuit of your goal – a commitment to excellence – that will enable you to attain the success you seek."
Mario Andretti

A few idea-rich customer service tips:

• When you **say thank you**… look your customers in the eyes and 'smile'. People are so seldom honestly thanked it will help drive home that you are grateful for their trust and business. You should be! After all, their purchase pays your bills and allows you to take care of your family and enjoy your life, doesn't it?

• **Offer your ongoing assistance.** Make sure they don't leave without at least two of your business cards. Remind them you'd appreciate them passing along your name to any of their friends or family who might also be in the market for _____. Word of mouth is a powerful marketing tool… if you prime them to use it.

• **Remind them of your firm's commitment to them and your guarantees.** Ask them to call 'you' if they have any questions. Don't use the word, *'problems'* or say, *'If something goes wrong',* as that could prime the pump for returns. Be proud, positive, and supportive of what you sell.

• If you have worked up a package for them and they did not buy the whole deal, **remind them you will keep their information on file** for future use. Let them know you'll let them know about special sales and events coming up. This primes the pump for a follow up call from you or an invitation to come in again. It also allows them to re-consider and add-on later.

• **Make sure you keep in touch.** One opportunity might be a quick call to see how they like their new "_____", after it is delivered or set up.

• **Walk them to the door and offer your hand.** This is a great time to personally say thanks again for coming into your store.

• **Help them to their car if they take purchase with them.** Go the extra mile.
• **Invite them to drop back** in and tell you how their purchase is working out. Maybe tell them, *"I'd love to hear from you"*. Again, use your electronic customer file to keep in touch and keep them informed of events and sales that would benefit them.

- **Give them a small gift or perhaps a coupon** for a coffee and/or Danish on you at a local coffee shop. (More so if they have just made a substantial purchase.) Perhaps you can make arrangements with one close to your store to do so.

- Since you have their name and address, why not **take 'one' minute to pen a handwritten thank you note** (not a form or routine) and drop it in the mail on your way home. Drop another business card inside it too.

Challenge

How can you reinforce good decisions and set the foundation for future service? This might be a good topic of conversation with your fellow team members.

- Perhaps when you are having a coffee or on that 'rare' occasion when you are standing talking to each other at the back of the store. Or, if you meet with colleagues (even from other businesses) from time to time.
- Come up with specific ways you can demonstrate or reinforce that your customer made a good decision.
- Come up with specific ways to generate future service and additional business or referrals.

A personal touch works!

"One of my clients is an older woman who is intimidated by technology. I have been trying to teach her, step by step, how to access her email and download attachments so she could listen to some meditation mp3s which I had sent her. I could tell she was struggling, so when I mailed her a hard copy of my next invoice, I surprised her by including a CD that I had burned of the meditations so that she could listen to them on her portable CD player. She was thrilled.

The lesson I got from this is that, regardless of how easy something may seem to me, it's how the *client* sees it that's important. If I can find a way to make it easier for my client to follow through with our work, it's my responsibility to do so."

© *Rachel S. Heslin www.thefullnessofyourpower.com*

How to turn their 'initial' purchase into repeat business

Most sales driven organizations are so preoccupied getting 'new' customers; they pay little attention to their existing customers. It is an expensive mistake when you let them 'slip away' as you have essentially just wasted your money and your efforts in getting them in the first place.

You see, by investing time on generating repeat business from your existing customers you and your company will reap the following benefits:

- You save on advertising costs to get a new customer in the first place
- They need your product/service, so they are your continuing target market.
- You can have a more effective mail out for follow up contacts and add on sales.
- You can ask them what they want and then you seek to satisfy them
- If they are happy with you and your organization, they will tell others – the power of word-of-mouth.
- You can make your existing customers an offer which can include their friends and colleagues.

Because your firm has already spent a substantial portion of your advertising money on attracting a new customer; it makes good sense (and dollars too) to work at keeping that customer once they have made a purchase.

"I think there is something more important than believing: Action! The world is full of dreamers, there aren't enough who will move ahead and begin to take concrete steps to actualize their vision."
W. Clement Stone

For your sales career to grow and be successful, you need to ACT to develop a growing relationship with your existing customers, so they understand that your business is looking after them. If they have already bought from you then they are your target market – so don't forget them. The chances are (70% according to a Harris Interactive survey), if they are happy with your business, they will buy from you again. They just need reminding of the benefits that your business can offer them.

Remember, out-of-sight leads to out-of-mind which can lead to out-of-business.

What does it cost you to acquire a 'new' customer? Ask your CFO or Store Manager for this figure: $_____ Often that figure is 6-7 times the cost of keeping a current customer and expanding the business they do with you.

Challenge: To help you measure your potential to secure repeat business, ask yourself these questions:

1. How good is your personal and your company's customer service?
2. Have you got systems in place to ensure consistency of service and product development?
3. Are you happy with your image – are you relaying the 'right' message?
4. What does your organisation do for customers that your competitors are not doing?
5. Do you make the most of the testimonials from your satisfied customers to keep the momentum going?
6. Do you have promotional activities in place which targets your existing customers, and which makes them 'feel' valued and special?
7. Do you survey your existing customers to help expand or improve your product or service to them?

So, how did you rate? Believe it or not there's much more to know when it comes to maximizing your sales potential for repeat business. Keep your existing customers coming back for more and getting them to 'spread the word' about your business.

It's always the little things that matter

When I attained my CAE, certified association executive, my boyfriend took me to dinner at Canlis. The owner came out to congratulate me early in the meal. Later they sent the dessert with my name and CAE in chocolate on the plate; that was incredibly customized beyond expectations, and I loved it.

I also worked an event where we had a team building exercise that was to paint a piece of artwork. I was flying the next day. When the venue was made aware, they offered to ship my piece complimentary. Little thing, I know they had to go out of their way to do and I loved the attention to detail.

© *Holly Duckworth, CAE, CMP www.leadershipsolutionsintl.com*

How to Up Sell for Increased Sales and Commissions
…and to better serve your customers

One of the secrets to your business success as a professional is effectively handling up selling or add-on business. It is one thing to get the order or sale; it is better to 'biggie-size' that sale. Often for you and the customer this is the best deal! It is a more profitable use of your time, for sure.

As a Professional – remember you are there to 'help' your customers make informed decisions that serve them. Real profits occur when your assistance 'allows' your client to purchase a larger or more expensive product or service, which 'better meets their needs!'

Up selling is easier when you consider your main business as 'sincerely' helping your customers. As you may have heard, being a 'trusted advisor' is the key. Think about the problems your customers encounter. What does it REALLY take to assist them and to solve their problems? That's your job!

Chances are your customer needs 'substantially' more than the simple inexpensive solution or purchase they first consider when approached. By grouping together several different products and services, you can give the customer a more comprehensive, relevant, or advanced package that goes further toward creating a long-term satisfying solution.

Sometimes you need to suggest a 'superior' version of a product that will better fit the needs or has the capacity to grow with their changing needs. It might be more expensive now, but it will be cost effective in the long run. The foundation for this approach is laid when you invest time finding out their needs and concerns, 'prior' to showing them specific products. They will thank you for being a true professional and not just selling them what they ask for. They will appreciate you allowing them to buy what they need and what will best suit those needs over the long haul.

Two simple ways to make Up Selling/Add-ons automatic and easy for the client/customer

Here are two field proven ways to build up selling/add-ons into any purchase. Use these and client/customers will often buy two or three times as much without giving it much thought. Many professionals have seen their sales double and triple simply by incorporating these simple techniques into their normal selling process and conversations.

Bundle, design group, or package several related or complementary products or services together. Set the 'package' price below what the total would be if the customer bought all the products separately.

When a customer inquires about a single item, investigate what they need and then educate him or her that they can get that item, PLUS a great deal more by purchasing your bundle, design group, or special package. Make sure you leverage off this design advantage for additional sales.

You will find many customers just can't resist a bargain. Announce your new bundle, design group, or package deal with flair.

"It works fine by itself, but it REALLY works when you add THIS!" If your product or service works much better with a complimentary or plug-in item or support items, be sure to tell customers about it. That is both good customer service and great salesmanship.

It is surprising how many products and services go hand in glove. It's hard to have one without needing the other. If it makes 'their' job easier or meets their unspoken needs, you are acting as a true professional by offering them a series of options. Professionals selling electronics (computers, etc.) know to ask if you need extra cables, connections, or companion pieces to allow your central purchase to work to your benefit.

I remember having to make a second trip into Edmonton (a 45-minute drive – each way) to pick up a cable for a new printer. I was not pleased to find out I needed a special one. My salesperson could have simply suggested it for me when I purchased the printer.

Successful up selling/add-ons needs to be at the core of every business or professional practice. It can instantly multiply your production, commissions, and profits. You might well go from just getting by, to living comfortably and from living comfortably, to rolling in wealth from happy customers earning you larger commissions.

Challenge: How familiar are you with your opportunities to assist your customers by up selling them or suggesting add-ons? Ask your senior consultants for help to enhance your expertise to better serve them.

If you are truly a professional and committed to helping your customers get what they need, you will create the opportunity to demonstrate that commitment on a regular basis. People will respond and reward you with additional orders. They will remember you and refer you to others who can use your products or services. **That's a triple win in my books.**

Rules of Value-Added Service

Understanding a few principles behind the concept of **value-added service** will help you and your team with the necessary changes to become value leaders in your respective fields and markets. Take a few minutes to think these through and discuss with your team. Discuss what needs to change to make them a strategic reality.

Customer satisfaction is 'relative' to your performance and their expectations.

Customer satisfaction is a very subjective thing to measure. It really is a matter of perception and experience. If you meet or exceed the 'unsaid – unwritten' expectations of your customers their perception will be a positive one. Fail to meet these expectations and you will find them less than satisfied or happy with you. One method to make sure you meet or beat these 'unsaid - unwritten' expectations is to do some research. Often, within an industry there are certain expectations which serve as the norm. Make sure you know what they are and use them as the bottom line in your service and performance. If you would succeed, make sure you go well past the 'normal' expectations.

There is some business you don't want – but you do want every opportunity.

When you first start in business or start a business you want to deal with everyone. This works for the short-term, but not over the long term. Hard as it seems, you need to fire some clients if the business they bring in is not profitable to you. Studies have shown that, on average, 80% of your business will be generated from 20% of your customers.

Additionally, trying to be all things to all people is a sure-fire way to go broke. You cannot effectively service or supply everyone. You need to decide early on what business you are in and what you can provide 'profitably' to your customers. You can't service them if you're no longer in business. Customer service is a long-term investment in your business.

Not all customers are valid targets for a value-added effort.

As you develop and reinvent your business you will need to decide which customers you can service profitably. Profit is not a bad word – it is the lifeline of your business.

Profit is the differential between having a 'job' or hobby and a sustainable career or business. As you become increasingly clear on what business you are in and what you can profitably provide in the marketplace, you will be able to better target and serve your customers.

> **Price is less important when the relationship between the buyer and the seller is stronger.**

Think about your own experience. Other than for convenience or disposable goods, where do you shop? Would you drive across town to save a few dollars? How often would you continue to deal with someone even if they are a bit higher in price? Why is that?

Would you agree that often it is the way you are treated that makes a big difference? Would you also agree that often it is the small details than make the difference? How can you develop this type of relationship with your customers? What would have to change to make it work?

Value-added Service – some myths

VAS – applies only to very technical, complex, long sales situations.

Some people *actually* think this is true. Value-added service applies to every facet of your business. Customer service is not just 'a part' of your business. Customer service 'is' your business. Without value-added customer service, you may not remain in business for long. How does this apply to you and your firm?

VAS – applies only to 'product'.

Service based businesses depend on this to an even greater extent. What differentiates the service-based business is the performance or delivery of service and the relationship with the client. How does this apply to you and your company? How can you ensure you incorporate VAS into the service component as well as your product offering?

VAS – only management or product managers can offer it.

This is a very shortsighted view. The most successful businesses worldwide have empowered and enrolled their complete staff in the process of value-added service. They realize that each time they encounter a customer is **a moment of truth**. They also realize that, to the customer, in each case they are the company. How would this apply to you?

How would you incorporate this philosophy into your workplace and enroll everyone on your team in applying it? Value-added service is the foundation that prepares your company to grow profitably and successfully. Learn to apply it well!

Value-added Customer Service Solutions

This is an 'action step' if you are seriously committed to providing value-added service. It takes time to think about the potential problems your customers may encounter. It also takes time to repair and deal with the ones they encounter that you don't anticipate.

Wouldn't it be nice to plan, be ready to deal with any problems that crop up, empower your staff to deal directly with client, respond to their concerns, and, better yet, work to eliminate problems altogether? Well, maybe the problem elimination will take some time. But during that interim, let's work through helping your customers get the best use and service from what you provide. Or maybe just be willing to help them solve their problems by purchasing and engaging your firm to help.

Is there 'one' problem your customers have in common? This may be one they encounter with your service or product or a problem they bring to you, hoping to find a solution. Brainstorm some possible solutions to this problem. Which one is the 'optimum' solution to offer to your customer in the above situation? Why?

In life, we get paid in direct proportion to how effectively we solve our customers or employer's problems. **How do you make yourself more valuable?**

Quite simple really! Make sure you are a person who allows their creativity to emerge to help people solve their problems, more so, with the follow up of selling and/or supplying something to a customer. Help them find and acquire what will best suit and meet their needs.

The true value-added client/customer service focused businessperson anticipates problems and works in advance to find the best alternatives for them. Is your firm one of these? What would need to change to make you a leader in Customer Service in a very competitive, global market, or more importantly, closer to home?

Take advantage of growth opportunities

Business at its essence is based on innovation, solving problems, value-added service; fulfilling the needs, wants, and desires of our clients. Here's a potpourri idea-rich sampler of how to take advantage of opportunities to build or unlock your business potential by adding to the options, services, and product mix you offer your customers.

- **What business are you REALLY in?** Keep asking this question and keep adapting your business to keep it fresh. Hint: think in terms of customer benefits. What do your customers get when they deal with you? What do they really want?

- **Combine two or more products or services** to create a new one. Perhaps you can work with a strategic partner or ally to develop a new service or product that will bring mutual benefit?

- **Take an idea from another industry** and transfer it or adapt to suit yours and the needs of your clients. (For example: air miles/coffee cards/buy 10 get one free promotions.) Now we have an App for that!

- **Try something that didn't work the FIRST time.** It might now; with changes in technology, resources, client needs, and attitudes.

- **Take advantage of the trends** or changing interest in the marketplace. This is where your customer service focus will help, a lot!

- **Use a different material or process** to do a traditional job. Creativity counts – actually, it can multiply!

- Look for ways to be a **value-added** company or person, focusing on real customer service. How can you personally make changes to what you bring to your work?

Being creative is often as simple as being willing to risk by trying new or unfamiliar things and activities. Creativity is what solves your problems and builds your long-term business. Looking at your business with fresh eyes and from different perspectives is one secret to **delivering true value-added customer service.**

Innovate or evaporate – The time to act is NOW!

When would be the best time to start some serious work on innovation in your team and organization to better serve your clients and customers? **Now, is the short answer!** The gap between imagination and achievement or actualization has never been shorter. Beginning 'somewhere' is always preferable to waiting while your team weighs the options and while the organization goes bust or gets left in the dust by those competitors who are being innovative and creative in this volatile market.

Author of *'Leading the Revolution',* **Gary Hamel** advocates *'radical innovation is the competitive advantage of the new millennium'*. With the aftermath since 9 - 11, 2007-08 meltdown; and a general shake up in our economy, Afghanistan, Arab Spring, Iraq, Crimea, a wake-up call is certainly in order.

But that can be a challenge to productive change with some organizations mental constraints and stuck in the mud mindsets. **J.K. Galbraith**, noted economist once shared, *"Faced with the choice of changing one's mind and proving there is no need to – almost everyone gets busy on the proof."*

Everyone needs to be involved. Partial commitment to innovation is commitment to failure. There needs to be a willingness to listen to and act on the change plan that comes from this innovation process.

Creative Partners' **Andy Radka** shared the results of a survey of 500 top American CEO's. They were asked what their organization needed to survive in the 21st Century.

- Their top answer was *"to practice creativity and innovation"*.
- However, *"only 6% of them believed they were tackling this effectively"*.

Quite a gap between stated needs and application. Obviously blending in a spirit of innovation takes time vs. a quick fix or special seminar. If innovation and creativity are so important, even critical in business survival, I wonder why the gap in application and implementation?

While each organization is distinct and different, there needs to be a more holistic, integrated approach to innovation and creativity as a culture. We need to get buy in on all levels. Further, we need to consider some important points to increase the possibility of idea generation, which in turn drives innovation and creativity in an organization.

What can you do to facilitate this process within your team? Here are some areas of concern in building a foundation for success under this creative and innovative initiative:

Innovation strategy: Innovation needs to be an 'integral part' of all strategies and policies in your organization, not just 'tacked' on as a quick fix up.

It needs to permeate every department and every section. Every employee must make it a focus in part as they do their respective roles. For example, how much time is spent in the boardroom discussing ongoing innovation strategy? This is where the 'rubber hits the road' and your employees see just how much you are committed to this path of action.

Support from top management: In too many organizations, ideas and innovation steps are already at risk at their inception.

Poor leadership can look the other way **or** take the courageous step and stretch out a helping hand to buoy them until they can be worked out and tried in the real world.

Ask yourself, *"Do my managers see themselves as leaders whose role is to* **'clear the way' for creativity** *or are they simply status quo oriented?"* Your employees and colleagues are watching for your leadership in this arena.

What will your employees see when they 'observe' your leadership?

Collective mindsets: Whether we acknowledge it or not we each have mindsets comprised of beliefs, attitudes, and values that drive or motivate our behaviour.

These collective mindsets (e.g., 'can't teach old-dogs new tricks' or 'my people aren't creative') frequently form barriers to the creative process. They need to be unlocked and unblocked.

Business guru **Peter Drucker** once said, *"…defending yesterday – i.e., not innovating – is far riskier than making tomorrow."* Make sure your organizational mindset is not creating an 'immune system' or anti-virus system that automatically rejects or attacks new ideas, processes, or challenges to the status quo business model. This can be your largest obstacle in embedding creative approaches and applied innovation within your organization.

Employees get tools and training: Are your staff given the tools and the on-going training they need to support a creative climate and innovation?

People and training are crucial to your success and the training needs to be ongoing and reinforced.

Creativity will not magically flourish with the advent of a few courses or the provision of a 'few' creative tools to a 'few select' people. Everyone needs to be trained and supported in his or her evolution of understanding and applied learning.

Knowledge management tools: Does your organization have an intranet that capitalizes on the stride's information technology has brought to the battle for business survival?

I.T. (information technology) often acts as an enabler, which allows us to break the traditional barriers of function, geography, and even hierarchy. This allows for internet-based sparking of ideas and a chance to engage and bring 'all' the minds or your various teams into the game. This is how you win! *For example: A few years back, the Titleist (golf company) used 5 of my articles on a new intranet site being set up for their sales staff across the US.*

What gets measured gets done – metrics for innovation: Creativity and innovation can be measured and, if so, are done on a more consistent basis. If creativity is rewarded, even more! Intellectual assets can impact heavily on your market value. Consider the differential and costs between hardware and software values.

Creation of an idea pipeline: Is there an effective innovation process or pipeline or some form of tracking system for converting ideas into innovative services or new products?

Is everyone on your team committed to feeding this process or pipeline? Only systematic processes, which incorporate a blend of logical and lateral thinking tools can bring creativity and innovation.

What are you doing to ensure you 'prime the pump' and keep this pipeline full and flowing?

Supplier and customer mindsets: Organizations create a demand for innovative suppliers to be able to serve their clients who are demanding innovative products and services.

Ask yourself, *"Are your current (and potential) clients able to support a dialogue about inventing your shared future?"* How about your suppliers and allied professionals?

They may not even recognize the future until they see it or are made aware of its possibilities. That, in part, is your job in the connection and education process of business.

Just a few thoughts to consider as you follow your quest to increased creativity and applied innovation in your organization. The time to act is now! Innovate or evaporate in the dust of those competitors who saw the need, made the investment, and took the lead. **It's your choice!**

Break-out-of-the-box Thinking

This will jog your problem-solving skills. You can create novel ideas by **NOT** following expectations, rules, regulations, assumptions or long-standing traditions, or company history or policy.

Just for a moment, remove the speed limits from your mind and challenge your traditional linear thinking. Ask yourself a few questions to trigger your creative juices.

Just a few *mind joggers* to help kick start your creative thinking.

Ask yourself: What if? If only? Why not? Who says? Does it apply to me? By whose standards? Is there another way? Let's pretend for a minute we had all the resources, personnel, and time? Is there a second right answer? What happens if I do nothing? What is the best that can happen? What is the worst that can happen? How can I benefit or learn from this experience?

Take a few minutes and write some answers that relate to your goal or problem at hand as they relate to the above statements.

Using this style of questioning process helps 'unlock your creativity'. It is this creativity that holds the seed of your eventual success in reaching your goal or resolution of your problem.

For more ideas on how to tap into your creative genius and unleash your creativity in your leadership and organization get a copy of 'Why Didn't I THINK of That?' by Bob 'Idea Man' Hooey from www.SuccessPublications.ca

Thinking in Reverse to Move Ahead

When setting your goals, **Steven Covey** suggests that we should **"begin with the end in mind"**. Wouldn't solving this problem be a worthy goal? Focus on the end or desired result. Take your time and define it carefully. Ask questions that eventually lead you carefully, step by step, back to the current state of affairs or situation. In business, it is called reverse engineering, but it works every time.

Define your ideal solution or desired outcome. Be as accurate as you can.

Keep asking yourself, "If this is the case, what would have to happen to get this result?" and use that as your next reverse step. Usually, you will find the path within 10 to 12 steps. Try it, you might just enjoy it!

1. _____ Ideal solution or desired outcome
   2. _____ next step (backward)
      3. _____next step (backward)
         4. _____next step (backward)
            5. _____next step
               6. _____next step
                  _____present

But sir, it's my duty to show you!

I visited an authentic Indian store while speaking in Mumbai. After touring we were brought into a seating area and given tea. A very nice man started bringing out trays of jewellery: diamonds, emeralds, etc. He asked if I liked them and then proceeded to bring out more trays. Wow!

I made the attempt to let him know I wasn't going to buy any. His response was to shrug and say, "But sir, it is my duty to show you!" Twice! Then I made the mistake of asking if he had any garnets. Why not look?

PS: My wife loved the box cut garnet earrings and matching garnet necklace I gave her for her birthday the next week when we met in Paris on my way home. Service works! © *Bob 'Idea Man' Hooey*

The 10 Pitfalls of Customer Service

Our customers look to us for guidance and all too often don't get what they expect. Instead, they get excuses or put-offs, when we should be giving them real service. Each customer engagement is an opportunity to make them feel special and enhance their relationship with you.

Think about the following 'killer' phrases – ever heard them? Ever heard them in your store or business? Here are a few thoughts on how I'd suggest you might better serve your customers.

We don't have that...
Might I suggest that a value-added service-based answer would be to find out what they need and offer to help them find it or direct them to where it can be found, even from another store! Service doesn't have boundaries and it is willing to go beyond the normal needs to help solve customers' problems.

All sales are FINAL!
This can all too often be a shortsighted policy if we are really service oriented and want the best for our customers. Many progressive companies have developed a liberal return and refund policy. Employees are empowered to assist clients as needed without calling in a manager.

I don't know who does that?
If we are genuinely service focused, we get the opportunity to act as a resource to finding what they need. Often a few calls or just being aware of what other people offer can be an immense service to clients. Who do you think they remember down the road? Becoming a resource increases your on-going value to potential clients and employers.

That's not my department!
Be willing to help – even when it isn't your department. Foster a sense of teamwork by taking leadership in making sure all your firm's customers are taken care of, not just the ones in your department.

Being all things to all people – YES!
On the other side of the coin, saying yes can be equally bad in trying to serve your clients. Being realistic about what you can feasibly deliver or have the depth of knowledge to share can be counterproductive. True customer service is in knowing what you can do well and directing clients to other suppliers for areas that fall outside your expertise.

Sorry, that's our policy!
Clients don't want to hear about your 'policy' – they want to hear how you'll help solve their problems. Flexibility in policy is essential if you are seriously committed to 'exceptional' customer service.

Tell us what you think... but you don't really mean it.
When you ask your clients for feedback – and that's a great idea – make sure you listen and acknowledge their input! Nothing will kill your credibility quicker than asking and then ignoring their responses. Build-in feedback opportunities and then respond to those who take the time to really tell you how you or your staff is doing. They are giving you valuable information. Take the time to thank them. Ask for their email address or other contact information and respond!

Call us about our special offer... but not everyone knows what it is.
Ever have a sale or in store special and forget to let everyone on your team know the details? Kind of embarrassing when your own staff is caught unaware of what the public knows or wants. Make sure everyone is on the same page when you market a special product, price, or service.

It will be ready tomorrow! You hope?
This is a big risk! Make sure you know what you are promising can be delivered on time, every time. In fact, be conservative in your estimation of delivery time and allow a margin for error and delays.

I don't know?
Not knowing is ok. Unfortunately, too often I hear this used as an excuse to not help your customers. If you don't know, make a point of trying to find out and tell your client you'll get back to them with the information.

If you are aware of these pitfalls in customer service and have a game plan to counter the negative impact of using them, you're part way there. Good customer service is systematically working to eliminate these pitfalls from your business and your vocabulary. Maximized customer service incorporates the following guiding principles.

Apologize, when necessary, but don't debate.
Customers will have problems and sometimes you will make mistakes. Apologize when necessary and make them happy. Don't enter into debate with clients – you never win. Be patient and listen. Then take care of their problem as best you can.

Feedback will keep you focused.
Making good use of feedback from your customers will help keep you focused on making your business work more effectively in serving clients.

Remember to stay adaptable and be flexible.
Business success is a process not perfection. Serving your clients' real needs will keep you flexible in your service, products, and procedures. It will build solid relationships too!

Always say yes or help them find it.
Being in business makes you in part a resource center for your clients. If you aren't able to solve their needs, make sure you know and can direct them to someone who can.

Under promise – always over deliver.
Make this one your bottom line in establishing and building your business. Proving your ability to serve your clients depends on your ability to deliver what you promise. Be clear about what you can deliver and when - and then move heaven and earth to make good on your promise.

Customer service is not just 'A PART' of your business. Customer service 'IS' your business! Without it – you will have no business.

Follow-up is essential if you want to succeed in business

If you want to be successful, you need to build a system to follow-up with all your customers. Do you realize the average business only hears from 4% of their dis-satisfied customers? According to **Lee Resources**, 91% of unhappy customers will not 'willingly' do business with you again. However, resolve their concerns or complaints in their favor and 70% will give you another chance and deal with you again.

This is where surveys and call backs are essential. If you wait for them to let you know of a 'problem', you will lose their business forever. Check to see what people are saying about you on-line (e.g., Twitter, LinkedIn, Facebook, etc.). This 'unfiltered' customer feedback on their experience can be invaluable to the smart business professional. If you are aware of a problem, you have the chance to do something about it and prove you really want to serve them. The fun part: when you fix their concern, many of them move into being raving fans and champions for you.

Five successful techniques for generating increased sales, repeat business, and engaging customers

Funny thing, as top performing professionals we need to consistently improve on our sales success. **There is no static in selling!** We need to be working on gaining new customers, repeat business, and of course, referrals just to keep current, let alone move up to the next level. Let's explore five field-proven success techniques you can use to generate an increase in your sales. You'll find them simple to use and effective for building any business.

Adding Something 'New' or improved to 'The Mix'

Every time you add something 'new' to your business, products, or service mix you create another new opportunity to get more sales. Each time you make a tweak or improvement you open a door for new client conversations. For example, something as simple as adding new information on your web site creates another selling opportunity when prospects and customers visit your site to access or view the new information. When was the last time you updated your web pages and, at least, changed the dates?

Adding a new product or service to the list of those you already offer can produce a big increase in sales. Even refreshing in-store displays help. The added service or product can increase your sales opportunities in three different ways:

- It attracts 'new' customers who were not 'initially' interested in your current products and services.
- It generates repeat sales from 'existing' customers who also want to have your new product or services.
- It enables you to get 'bigger' sales by combining 2 or more items into special package or bundle offers.

Become a Value-added Resource to Your Customers

Look for ways you can be a trusted resource for your prospects and customers. Supply them with relevant, free information on how to do something more effectively, enhance their business, or save money. Be able to refer them to allied professionals who can help them in areas you don't cover or provide. You get another opportunity to sell something every time they come back to you for help. This enhances your credibility and builds a trust relationship. *For example, with our Secret Selling Tips we added a weekly Motivational Sales Quotes service.*

Separate Yourself from Your Competition

Find or create a reason for customers to do business with you instead of with someone else offering the same or similar products or services. What makes you 'unique'? For example, do you provide faster results, easier procedures, personal attention, or a better guarantee?

Determine the unique sales/service proposition (USP) or competitive advantage you offer to clients/customers that your competitors do not offer. Promote that advantage/benefit in all your advertising. Give your prospects valid reasons to do business with you instead of with your competition, and you'll automatically get more sales.

Focus and Promote the Result

Your customers don't really want your product or service. They want the benefit produced by using it. They don't really care about your background, your services, or even your products. What they 'really' care about are the 'results' they get from using you instead of someone else.

For example, car buyers want convenient transportation with a certain image. Business opportunity seekers want personal and financial freedom for themselves and their family. Sales Managers want successful programs (like *'Secret Selling Tips'*) that will help equip and motivate their sales teams to be more profitable in the selling game. Make sure your web pages, sales letters, other sales materials, or media are promoting the result or true customer benefits your customers really want and need.

Anticipate and Prepare for Change

Change is the biggest challenge to your sales or business success. The days are history when a business could constantly grow by simply repeating what it did successfully in the past... or even recently. Aggressive, innovative, global competitors and rapidly changing technology make staying with the status quo impossible if you want to survive.

Think about some larger well-known firms that are in trouble or have gone out of business. In most cases, their 'failure' was primarily due to ignoring changes in technology, customer needs, competition, and changes in the market or other factors that might have been incorporated into their working environment. If they'd been awake, and willing to change, they might still be profitable. Now they are dead or near dead!

Expect change and actively prepare for it. Don't wait until your income declines to act. Develop the habit of looking for early warning signs that something is changing. Then confront it aggressively before you start to lose customers.

Hint: Insure yourself against the impact of change by increasing the number of complementary products and services you offer and by using a variety of different marketing methods. Only a small portion of your total business will be affected if the sales of one product fall off or the response to one marketing method declines. Always be adjusting what you do to be more effective in finding and keeping your customers.

How many of these five field-proven techniques have you overlooked or ignored? How many of these are currently being used in your selling or business strategies? When will you act on some new ones?

Good customer service can be a great way to say you're sorry

Many years ago, I had to take my car in for some routine repairs. I had dropped it off when the garage opened and been told it would be ready by the end of the afternoon. Working as a TV news anchor, my days were unpredictable, action packed, and featured very little free time. I'd moved heaven and earth to find the time to pick up my car.

That's when disappointment entered the picture. Even though my car's repairs were routine, and the garage had it for the whole day, the work still wasn't done. The service manager apologized. I wasn't interested in excuses due to a pressing problem, *"I have to be on live TV in less than 45 minutes. I need a car."* I was immediately put into a loaner. I pulled out feeling frustrated and defeated.

The next day, I still felt angry when I picked up my car. The service manager apologized again and then surprised me. *"I noticed that one of your door handles was broken so we replaced it,"* he said. *"I also fixed one of your windows, which wasn't going up and down very smoothly. We wanted to apologize for not having your car done yesterday and I hope these 'free' repairs help."*

In a moment, my feelings changed. The two repairs were little problems that I hadn't mentioned but bugged me daily. I now realized that my first experience with the garage had been an exception and **not** the rule. Not every business can be perfect every day. But it can make things right if it ever falls below expectations.

© Ken Okel www.okel.com Used with permission of the author

Getting your customers to sell you…
Creating fans and champions

Over the years, I have discovered, quite by accident that my best investment in building my sales and business was in taking very good care of my existing clients/customers. When they are happy and more than satisfied with my products or service, they will talk about me to their friends and colleagues.

Some will even go the extra mile to becoming fans or champions and firmly telling their friends and colleagues that they 'must' deal with me if they want the best value or service. Wow! Often, they have been instrumental in garnering new business for me as they excitedly share their success or satisfaction with their colleagues and friends.

> **Secret Selling Tips…**
>
> I had lunch with the CEO of a large Canadian retail firm I had worked with for a number of years, training their VPs, helping create a book to reinforce their culture, as well as writing for their internal magazine.
>
> As we came to the finish of our lunch, **Kim Yost** mentioned he needed to find a way to help his 1500 salespeople become more effective, focused, and profitable. We dialogued some ideas and in less than 15 minutes had outlined the basic idea for what would become **Secret Selling Tips on-line program.** We launched the English version a month later and the French one shortly after that.
>
> I had approached this as a way to serve this particular leader, who had become a good friend. What I didn't see was this customer service focus would lead to a completely new on-line business for us. He invited me to share what we'd done with 9 of his counterparts south of the border and 4 of them signed up their entire sales teams too. Wow! This simple service idea started generating $30-50K a year.

Go the extra mile – inspired action to separate yourself from your competition

One of the most effective activities in building loyalty and turning customers into repeat buyers, raving fans, and champions of your service or business is to go the extra mile. By this I mean doing more than would be normal to help them achieve the success or satisfaction they wanted.

- Have you ever experienced having someone going way past what would normally be included in your purchase?
- Did it catch your attention and make you take notice?
- How can you do this with your customers?

Do the unexpected – truly amaze them

Companies have the opportunity to build amazing relationships and repeat business. Yet so few are successful.

- How many times have you been positively surprised in dealing with a salesperson or company?
- They gave you more than you expected or did something you thought would be an extra?
- How did you feel?
- How can you do that in your business?
- Are there some small value-added areas or 'extras' that you can incorporate into your service or product mix?
- How about including some items that other competitors charge extra for or don't offer at all?
- Do you think that would help to create a positive experience in the minds of your clients?

Follow up for complete satisfaction – part of the sales process

One of the areas for growth in providing real value-added service is in the follow-up or follow-through. How frequently have you had someone you'd dealt with call you a while later to see how you like your purchase and checking to see how it's working? Sadly, too many salespeople miss a great opportunity to build profitable long-term relationships, by simply following up with prospects or existing clients.

Customer service is pro-active and deals with the little 'adjustments' before they become major irritants. I think we're too scared of the possibility of hearing negative comments or having to go out to fix something. How sad!

The very thing that can turn customers into loyal fans and we're afraid to do it. Many of the most successful companies have a 100% complete satisfaction – whatever it takes policy. Do you? How will you incorporate this area of customer service into your process?

Keep in touch – top of mind means additional sales and business

On a parallel path, how many companies can you think of that have taken the time to keep in touch with you after you've finished paying for the service or product? Sadly again, very few!

Part of building a positive relationship and turning customers into loyal fans and enthusiastic champions can be simply taking a positive step to keep in contact. How can you build in an easily maintained system to allow you to track your customers? How will you find ways to keep in touch? What commitment will you make to ensure it gets done?

Challenge
Take a moment and think of some other ways that will help you build those relationships that turn your customers into repeat buyers, fans, and champions. Are there any opportunities you've missed to establish this mutually beneficial type of customer relationship? It is never too late to do what is right and to ask for a second chance.

Keep in mind the potential lifetime value potential of your customers.

"Real excellence does not come cheaply. A certain price must be paid in terms of practice, patience, and persistence – natural ability notwithstanding." Stephen Covey

---

Create Space (Kindle) goes way beyond the basics

This is the 6th book we've done with **CreateSpace.com**, an Amazon company. They work hard at giving authors and publishers great service to help them get their ideas into print. (Now Kindle Plus)

Have a question? Go on-line and ask them to call you 24/7 and they connect within a minute to help you. Have a challenge like I did recently with one of our books? The package of proof copies arrived one short (not a biggie), but one of them had black spots that streaked when you rubbed them. I phoned to ask them about it and they explained what had happened. They told me they would ship me another complete order at their cost; 3 days later they arrived. Wow!

They have gone way beyond the basics on our behalf, and we love them for it. We confidently recommend them to our fellow authors, **Irene Gaudet** helps them get into print. **www.VitrakCreative.com** or through **www.SuccessPublications.ca**

So, you have a problem… that's great!

So, you have a problem, that's great! Some of you are thinking, "Are you crazy?" Actually… NO! Someone once told me **that I'd get paid or determine my value, by my ability to solve problems.**

If it was 'easy', everyone would be doing it, and the competition would be intense. But, as most clients/customers will tell you, most businesses are not in the problem-solving field. Your ability to solve your client's problems will be directly related to the number of sales and continued growth of your firm. The more successfully and **creatively you solve these problems**, the more referrals and fans you'll see. The more productive you are personally in being a solution-oriented owner, manager, or employee, the more dramatically it will affect your paycheck and career path.

I've learned a **simple 4-stage process for dealing with problems**. This is an effective way to deal creatively with customer complaints and concerns as well as other areas of your business and life. These ideas also work with creative and strategic planning or in everyday problem solving.

Since many of my clients and audiences have a need to be effective in dealing with their clients or customers, I've written from that perspective.

1. Invest time making sure you **UNDERSTAND** the problem.
2. The key to understanding is to **IDENTIFY** the real cause.
3. Take time to fully explore and **DISCUSS** possible solutions.
4. Act to **SOLVE** or resolve the problem.

'Idea-rich customer service' is a strategic commitment to go through this process with your clients. After the problem has been successfully resolved, **go the extra mile**. By that I mean doing something unexpected to assist the client or to show them you appreciate the opportunity to fix the problem and prove your commitment to his well-being. This will help turn an angry or frustrated client into a fan, or better yet… a champion for you and your business.

Stage One: Understanding the problem: often a problem is a perception of a difference of what we expected to happen and what happened. Here are 3 action steps to help.

1. Gather ALL the facts. Be thorough and investigate. Let the client talk!

2. Listen carefully and don't be defensive. Wait until they've finished talking and ask more questions to draw them out, to find out their REAL concerns.
3. Rephrase or repeat the problem back to the client to make sure you've heard it correctly and understand what needs to be resolved. Agree on this stage.

It's important at this stage to make sure you don't fall into the trap of denying or trying to avoid the problem. Or, worse yet, blaming or attacking someone else, or demonstrating the same negative emotions in response to a customer's complaint. Just listen and calmly gather the facts!

Stage Two: Identify the Cause of the Problem: You might ask yourself or your client a few questions to find out what may have caused the problem.

1. What has happened? Listen and ask questions. True assessment of current situation.
2. What should have happened? Ask questions and listen carefully. Was perception a problem?
3. What went wrong? This is where you start partnering with the client.

Keep in mind the true cost of an unhappy client. What future purchases could you expect from this client? What future business this client could influence? What does the problem at hand cost to rectify?

Problems generally often fall into 4 major areas:

1. **Mechanics or Function** – product or service failed to work as expected.
2. **Assembly or use** – someone didn't use it correctly or put it together incorrectly.
3. **The People Factor** – we make mistakes in how we do something or how we deal with a client.
4. **Client EGO** – how this PROBLEM makes them look (good or bad) in their eyes and the eyes of their friends and families.

Stage Three: Explore and DISCUSS possible solutions. This is possibly the most critical part in the client satisfaction/problem solving process. Here is where we need to fully focus and objectively look at the challenge, we've partnered with the client to solve. Here again are a few action steps.

1. Suggest options. Take time to explore ALL the options that might effectively help solve this problem or at least minimize the impact.

2. Ask your customer for their ideas. Very often, they have a solution in mind or have some good input that will help you mutually resolve it to their satisfaction. If they are a partner in the decision, they will help make it work and will be more inclined to be happier with the results. Their satisfaction will result in referrals for you!
3. Agree on the best solution or course of action. After you've fully explored the options, make sure you both agree on what and when you will do to resolve it. THEN DO IT!

Stage Four: Take ACTION to resolve the problem. This is the completion stage that builds a foundation for a potential long-term relationship with your 'formerly' dissatisfied client. Make this a priority focus for your firm. Once you've agreed on what needs to be done, move heaven and earth to do it, and do it better and quicker than you've promised.

Remember, they are watching to make sure you were serious about making them happy. This is your chance to prove your commitment. Again, three simple action steps.

1. Physically remove the cause of the problem and/or take steps to retrain if personnel based.
2. Take corrective action to substitute, replace, or repair the product or service.
3. Ask the client if they are satisfied with the changes and action you've taken.

Going the extra mile! This is where you cement the relationship by doing something extra, something totally unexpected by the client. Show them you care and are concerned about the inconvenience they've experienced.

Use your complaints as a source of product or service development. Each one is an opportunity for you to learn how to better serve your clients, refine your service, or improve your product in the marketplace. This is also an opportunity to expand your business or service by using solutions as steppingstones or business building blocks.

Yesterday's problems are today's new and improved products or services. Want to be a creativity leader? Then learn from each lesson your clients give you. This is an opportunity for you to build a strong foundation for success. **Don't miss the lesson. It might be a 'v-e-r-y' valuable one!**

A personal note from Bob

I trust we've been able to share some creative approaches to problem solving or strategic planning. I appreciate the opportunity to exercise my creativity and learn together with my audiences. Often, the lessons we discuss, and the ideas generated help me in refining my approach and my program content.

I would challenge you to use these tips and techniques in your day-to-day operations, as well as in your personal life. I think you'll find them helpful. **Remember there is always a creative solution!** Share these ideas with your clients and co-workers, so they can take advantage of ways to make their lives more productive and less stressful.

One of the challenges of speaking within a time frame and having a topic that has so many variables to discuss, is covering the most relevant material. That is one of the reasons for developing these books and learning guides to help my audience members following a presentation.

We refer to more problem-solving models in *'Why Didn't I THINK of That?'* Purchase a copy for future reference and focus on the ones that might serve you best as you begin to reframe your approach to problems that inevitably appear in your life and career. I hope you enjoy it.

Visit: **www.SuccessPublications.ca** for information how to get your personal copy.

Top reasons for client loss

1. **Customers feel they are treated poorly.**
2. **Failure to solve a problem.**

Harris Interactive uncovered a few points we, as smart businesspeople might want to take into consideration. According to a 2011 **Harris Interactive** survey, customer service agents failed to answer consumer's questions 50% of the time. Their questions, not even their concerns! 86% of consumers surveyed had stopped doing business with a company due to bad customer service.

You may not make them 'all' happy or answer their questions to their complete satisfaction, but you must be disciplined to make your best attempt to do so. Going the extra mile will pay off for you.

Turning Client Complaints into $ and sense!

Customer complaints can be a 'gold mine' if handled correctly and with the proper attitude and perspective. In fact, they can be an asset to helping you become more productive and profitable. Unfortunately, all too many businesses treat them with less than courteous responses and deal with them as quickly as they can.

Customer complaints and feedback offer:

- **Real (RAW) feedback on your performance.** Using this steady flow of feedback and information can be beneficial to adapting and keeping your business and its policies current and effective.

- **Complaints because they care.** It may not seem like it, but customers who complain are demonstrating they care about the relationship and the value you provide. They are also giving you an opportunity to show how much you care and value them. This is a chance to turn them into fans and champions by going the extra mile to take care of their needs.

- **Opportunity to refine your product mix and service.** People's problems, feedback, and complaints can be a mirror to show *cracks in your process* and areas where you can make changes to improve, refine, or adapt your service and product mix. Don't miss out!

- **Opportunity to see new areas of growth or expansion.** The successful business is always on the lookout for ways to expand their business by offering more to their clients.

- **Opportunity to be a leader in your field.** Each complaint is an opportunity to see areas for improvement in your business – to better compete and serve their needs. Leaders seize the opportunities and build on them. Are you a leader or an also ran?

- **Opportunity to prove your commitments.** We talk about customer service and taking care of business, a lot! But here is a great opportunity to prove firsthand to your clients and staff just how committed you really are to this area of service.

Remember: If you're not taking care of your customers, your competitors will!

Getting customer feedback using surveys

The most successful companies around the world take leadership in their customer service by asking their clients how they did. Acting on that information to improve or adapt their business process and operating policies is what makes them successful.

To be effective in this area it is very important to **keep the following principles in mind:**

- **Begin with clear objectives.** Be very clear on what you want to learn and in the questions you ask. Be specific and give clear instructions on how you want them to respond.

- **Give them a good reason for responding.** Bribery works – smile! But seriously, give them an 'incentive' or a 'reward' for taking their time to give you the valuable feedback you desire. A free offer, a special discount, a special gift. Something they would value – to give you value.

- **Ask questions that are important to them.** Ask questions from their perspective. Questions that would be important to their receiving better service, selection, or other area of importance. This is one time to really put yourself in their shoes and think accordingly.

- **Keep it brief.** People are busy – don't make your survey a chore – it won't get done. If it is brief, focused, and fun, they will respond. Remember: better done than perfect.

- **Confidential self-mailer surveys can generate higher responses.** There are times when allowing them to answer confidentially will get you what you want. If you are asking questions about your staff, make sure the responses are directed to you and that your clients know they will have your confidence.

- **Ask easy-to-answer questions.** Keeping in mind clients are busy – make your questions quick and easy to answer. A mixture of yes/no, rating 1-10, and open-ended questions will give you the answers you need.

- **Remember to thank them.** Gratitude goes a long way with people who help you.

- **Comments to encourage opinions.** A few comments from you along with the survey as to your reason to approach them and your commitment to better serve them will work wonders.

- **Test the survey before sending it out.** Just like testing your marketing and advertising, I'd suggest testing your survey on a few select customers before you send it out to everyone. Make sure the questions are clear to your customers and you will get the feedback and answers you really want. Revise and send it out.

- **Focus on your best customers.** Remember Parado's principle that 80% of your business is generated by 20% of your clientele. Find out from the clients who shop frequently or stay with you why they do so and what they'd like to see changed. They've already proven their commitment to your business and are more likely to give you honest feedback you can use. This will also engage them and draw them closer to you and your business. People like to help and be asked for advice.

- **Postcards sent in advance of the survey can arouse their curiosity.** One way of improving the response rate of your survey is to let people know the survey is coming. Perhaps tease them, 'just a little,' in advance of the actual survey arriving in their mail or email box. That way they've had a chance to think about the experiences they've had with you and subconsciously at least are prepared to respond to your request for feedback.

With the advent of online (free) survey tools (like Survey Monkey) it has never been easier to gain the information you need. Just make sure you have their emails and mention you might ask for their advice and insight from time-to-time.

Surveys are a great way to learn how to reinvent and keep your business fresh and viable. They are also a great way to discover ways to serve your clients more effectively.

"The handful of companies that respond promptly and accurately to customer emails increase trust in their brand, bolster customer satisfaction, and boost sales both online and offline." **Benchmark Portal**

Visit: www.SuccessPublications.ca/BusinessSuccess-Tips.html for special business building success video tips, just for you.

Mistakes Made by Newer (Sales) Staff

Why is it that senior sales staff are frequently *more effective and more productive* in their sales efforts? Could it be that they've learned these simple points that help them sell better? You work hard to either identify potential clients to call or to promote your business and its products and services to entice potential clients to visit. When your staff engages them how often do you see your efforts wasted as they walk out the door or say, "No Thanks!"?

The essence of true customer service is a solid commitment to providing them with the most professional sales and service possible. But there are some obvious pitfalls here as well.

1. **Lack of preparation.** There is an old saying: "Success happens when opportunity meets preparedness!"
2. **Not listening**. 90% of salespeople never listen and are doomed to ineffectiveness.
3. **Failing to ask for the order**. Most of the studies I've read show that 70% of all sales folks NEVER ask for the order. Do yours?
4. **Poor or no follow up**. Follow up and follow through is where 90% of all great sales are made.
5. **Small thinking**. Want bigger sales, bigger orders? You must think bigger. Ask these questions: "How high is high? What is my maximum potential?"
6. **Failing to establish and/or maintain rapport.**
7. **Failing** to really commit and establish themselves as experts in their field.

Ask yourself how you and your colleagues fare on each of these areas? Would you give yourself a passing mark? Which ones would need a little work? How will you change to make sure you give your clients/customers the most professional service possible?

Give your team a chance to win by reminding them of these success tactics. Remind them to keep focused and keep working toward their goals of helping the client make a decision that is good for the client and profitable for the company. How can you help them make the changes they need to become a professional salesperson and provide value-added service?

Creating TIME for effective training

Investing in continual training and professional development allows your team the opportunity to fully realize their potential. It pays big dividends on better-equipped, energized team players on the job. As a top-level leader and team coach this can be your biggest time challenge as well as opportunity for success.

Finding 'time' for your team members to attend training can be a challenge for most organizations. Applying creativity to your training program can yield powerful results in their sales and customer recruitment and retention.

These ideas will reduce 'excessive' classroom instruction time, without jeopardizing the process of quality face-to-face, interactive training

- Schedule team members to attend training between 10AM and 3PM, instead of a full day. In this case, they can still attend to urgent business and client follow up. This works best for on-site training or training held very close to your operation.
- Weekend seminars and retreats are increasing in popularity. However, if you ask your team to sacrifice their private time, be sure to include some group outing or banquet to show your appreciation. Trade-off time during the week would be nice too!
- Suggest your team study or read up on the course material in advance so they can hit the seminar running. Professional trainers can provide advance materials to facilitate this process.
- How about scheduling a 'lunch and learn' or 'breakfast briefing with Bob' by inviting in a local expert when your team needs information on a simple topic. Or combine a 'breakfast briefing' for management or specific team members in addition to half day or full day training.
- Visit: **www.BobHooey.training or www.ideaman.net** for more information on our idea-rich programs and materials to assist you in enhancing your career or leading your team.

How to avoid expensive training mistakes

As a leading-edge owner, executive, manager, or team leader you may be asked to make decisions to engage or contract on programs and policies that will either help or hinder your team in reaching their goals. You can avoid making major, career limiting, expensive training mistakes by considering a few ideas and side-stepping some of these mistakes that have minimized returns on training dollars.

Unfortunately training dollars can be ultimately wasted when leaders make some of the following mistakes. You can avoid them!

Failing to fully assess team needs

Perhaps you are teaching your team skills they already have? Team members don't need training 'just for the sake of training'. I've heard managers say, *"Even if they know this stuff – a refresher won't hurt them!"*

Sometimes that is true (I have been asked back to reinforce a program or to provide add-on sessions or coaching). If not handled correctly, it can be counter-productive to your end goals or de-motivating to your team.

Here's an idea-rich suggestion

Before you launch any training program, conduct a needs assessment with your team. Work to establish a 'comprehensive list of skills' of current team members. This way you may discover what they already know and what they need (and hopefully want) to learn. Then, as you provide training, it will send a 'positive' message that reinforces the idea that you value their contributions and are dedicated to helping them increase and hone their skills. Training can be perceived as a 'punishment or a perk' depending on how you position or frame it.

Strategically design your training programs to incorporate follow up reinforcement to enhance their effectiveness. Make that a vital part of your program and design it to ensure it is productive reinforcement not a perceived punishment. Let them know you are committed to their long-term growth and success in their roles.

Thinking (wishfully) that training sessions will eliminate conflict

Leaders and managers sometimes think that training, especially training that focuses on team or relationship building, will, in itself, eliminate conflict on the job. Some programs over emphasize teamwork at the expense of 'team-effectiveness'. All team efforts need to be focused, task and relationship oriented. When sessions focus 'too much' on relationship building vs. team-effectiveness they lose impact and may become counter-productive.

Team building is a very important aspect of any successful business or organization. Make sure it is not 'sacrificed' in replacement for 'team-effectiveness'. Professional leadership is being able to work with people who may 'bug you' and being able to direct their efforts to help the team succeed.

Here's an idea-rich suggestion

Work diligently to ensure everyone on your team understands that *constructive* conflict is an important part of the team process. Without some conflict and honest difference of opinion, you get mediocrity. As someone once told me, *"The opposite of conflict is apathy, not peace and harmony."*

The secret is in not taking conflict as a 'personal issue' or a negative result in the process. Creative, constructive conflict can be a 'strategic' part of a positive process in making sure your team makes the right choice and (time permitting) fully explores all the options and potential pitfalls.

Visit: www.legacyofleadership.ca/bonus.htm for a special gift to help you in your leadership journey.

Thinking of training as a program vs. an on-going process

One of the challenges in training is the expectation that a half-day, full day, or even a few days of training can change years of embedded habit. Research shows that shorter sessions, with reinforced follow-up, spread over a longer time result in better retention and long-range effectiveness. 'Short and often' rather than a one-time massive attack seems to work better. That is one of the reasons behind the success of our spaced online video coaching and training programs like *Secret Leadership Tips* or our *Speaking for Success* on-line coaching series.

Here's an idea-rich suggestion

For your training to be effective, insights and ideas gained during programs must be quickly translated into action (**Ideas At Work!**) – actions that are reinforced by the leaders on your team. Real self-development is never done, as is the true essence of education. In our live interactive sessions, audience members are challenged to make a specific commitment to act on what they learn and to schedule those actions.

Visit us at: www.ideaman.net or www.BobHooey.training for more information. We trust these suggestions will help you as you search out the most effective training programs for your team. We'd be happy to share some other thoughts with you if you have any other questions or queries. Of course, we'd be happy to explore how we might be of service in on-site or virtual training for you and your team.

*"I hear and I forget.
I see and I remember.
I do and I understand!"*
Confucius

These wise words were written thousands of years ago, and yet they ring true in lives and evolving business endeavors.

We 'best equip' those we lead with use-it-now information, practical tools and applicable actions, 'when we facilitate' them in getting their hands 'dirty' or getting up and using what we provide.

For example: In our *'Speaking for Success'* presentation skills training and executive speech coaching programs, the quicker we get the students or clients up speaking, the better they learn and accelerate their learning curve. Consider the thousands of Toastmasters around the world who nervously start speaking and find that their confidence and competence increases in direct relation to how often they are in front of an audience and in how they apply the feedback received. From years of experience, I know becoming an effective presenter is not learned 'exclusively' from a book or observing others in action. It is essentially a learn-as- you-do project. Kind of like life!

We work to incorporate hands-on or self-discovered learning and engagement in all our training programs. We've found this to be more impactful than an old-style lecture format. We've found when our students and audiences are having fun, being challenged, and engaging with each other, they tend to anchor the principles being taught. Our clients have found that their retention and application rates have improved too.

My challenge for you is to revisit what you are doing for your own learning curve, as well as those you work with... see where you can adapt it to add more *hands-on* experience. How can you make it more experiential to anchor the learning and enhance the skill?

"The rise of the citizen review site is a sobering development. No longer are you on top of the mountain, blasting your marketing message down to the masses through your megaphone. All of a sudden, the masses are conversing with one another. If your service or product isn't any good, they'll out you."
David Pogue, Scientific American, 2011

Proactive strategies to minimize price objections

Wouldn't it be great if price wasn't a factor with your clients? Reality check – it can be or perhaps it might not be the main factor if you work it right. How do you compete when you know you aren't the least expensive in your area? How do you compete in an increasingly competitive global and/or on-line market?

Here are a few areas that will help you and your team in this regard.

Strategic Value Analysis: Taking the time to find out a bit about these four areas will help you build a strong foundation and relationship to better service your customers. Better relationships will take the pressure of the price factor in the buying decision. The more you know, the better you can apply that knowledge in serving those who need what you provide.

- Market Analysis
- Competitive Analysis
- Self-analysis
- Customer Analysis

Positioning Strategies – to create barriers: Some of the more successful companies have carved out a position as the quality leader in their field. This emphasis on quality or value moves the evaluation process away from price.

Outsmart the competition: Use your brains and look for ways to better 'service' your customers. Find ways to provide services or value-added products that your competition doesn't.

Use all your resources: Being lean and mean in using your resources can help you keep your overhead in line and keep your pricing competitive. Using your resources fully allows you to better serve your clients as well.

Decide on all organizational needs: Taking time to streamline your operation. Keep it simple! This will help your staff provide the best service possible. It also allows your customers to see firsthand your commitment to giving them value for their dollar.

Work to generate end-user support: If you are in the position of being a supplier – your customers are really your customers' customers. How can you help your customers by working to reach and teach the end users? Become a drawing point for your customers.

Value-added Checklist What do you provide that has value for a potential client? List them now! (List 10 minimum – go for 20)

Bundling: How about making what you offer more valuable by combining products or services to allow your customers lots of options? What types of bundles can you offer?

Proactive probing: Take time to find out what moves your customers. What keeps them up at night? Ask questions and respond to what you learn, by adapting or changing your business. This is one way of keeping what you offer current, valuable, and viable.

Reinforce value: Everything you do should be focused on reinforcing the value in what you offer. What is the true value of what you offer? Warranty, service, selection, delivery, options?

Sell intangibles: Often the true value of what you sell is based on things that can't be shown or proven until needed, as above. Do you have a better warranty? Do you offer better terms? Do you offer a better selection or stocking? Do you offer expert advice or consulting? Do you offer delivery and installation? If so, let them know!

Presentation ideas: When you get an opportunity to present or share about your business or products – I'd suggest looking for ways to incorporate the following areas. You can be a great spokesman if you do. **How can you…?**

- Demonstrate earnings
- Cut their costs
- Go for agreement to product first
- Choose your words carefully
- Use proper sales terms instead of jargon
- Sandwich the price – focus on value (good, better, best!)
- Summarize price with benefits
- Cost as a 'mere' fraction
- Minimize the cost-to-own
- Analogize
- Use testimonials wherever possible
- Think and talk long-term
- Present in its best light

The above critical impact areas are essential to being a value-based customer service focused business. Look for ways to build them into your business.

The effort will pay off – BIG TIME!

Checkpoints for Super Sales Techniques

Here are some points to keep in mind as you re-enter the field of sales and negotiation with your potential clients. Please keep these checkpoints in mind, as they've been pulled from the tactics used by successful top salespeople in various fields. Making sure you focus on being ready to help your clients make informed decisions will make substantial improvements to your bottom line. It will also make a difference in gaining repeat clients and referrals. Learn and earn from the secrets of the professionals in your industry. We share some of these tips when doing sales training for our clients and their teams. They've found them helpful, hence why they are included here.

YOU and YOUR STAFF play a solid role in laying the groundwork for business success and sales.

- Be neatly groomed
- Smile sincerely
- Keep the work area neat
- Recognize the customer immediately

CARING is demonstrated and appreciated and effective in the business and sales process.

- Be sincere
- Engage a greeting that requires a positive response
- Focus on the customer and the merchandise
- Emphasize a genuine desire to serve

LISTENING is the secret tool used by the superstars – use it! See the following pages for more information on applying this business building success tool.

- Listen for the message behind the words
- Be aware of the customer's body language

TELEPHONE TIPS to build a professional image and support your business connection and sales. Voice connection is an important tool to client attraction and retention.

- Answer promptly and politely
- Put a smile in your voice
- Speak clearly
- Personalize the conversation

MERCHANDISE – being knowledgeable is the secret to being profitable and staying in business.

- Know what merchandise or services your organization offers
- Know where it is located or what is needed to apply it
- Know when and where it is available

BENEFITS/FEATURES – people buy what benefits them!

- Listen to the customer to find out what they consider to be product benefits or features of interest to them
- Sell the customer the product benefit supplemented with the product features

SELLING is both an art and an applied skill that can be honed and enhanced.

- Demonstrate products using a 'you' attitude
- Differentiate between excuses and objections
- Ask only positive questions when closing a sale
- Suggest complementary merchandise that will help the client

KNOW YOUR CUSTOMER to better serve and sell your customer.

- AIDA (attention, interest, desire, action)
- LEAR (listening, empathizing, asking questions, responding)
- Use 'what' questions to draw them out

Remember you are 'always' selling. Your company, its reputation, your services and guarantees, your selection and product mix, your staff expertise and friendliness, your ability to solve problems, and your willingness to go the extra mile to see that the client is satisfied.

Learn to Listen – A forgotten skill for business builders

Listening is the 'effective' business builder's forgotten communications skill. Active, strategic listening is the secret skill applied by top performing leaders and their teams. This is what you should have been given in grade one to help you succeed in school! Active listening will help you gain the 'edge' both personally and professionally in your communication efforts. Your business effectiveness will increase as you apply these skills. This customer service skill will help you and your team to enhance your productivity in business!

Some Listening Facts

If you are like most people, you spend approximately 60 percent of your workday listening. Like many of us, you probably retain only 25 percent of what you hear. In less than two months, most people generally recall only half of the 25 percent of the message they initially retained.

There is also a substantial difference between the average rate at which people speak (100 to 250 words per minute) and the time required by the average listener to process the message (400 to 500 words per minute.) This allows you to tune in and out of the message, which means you may miss the meaning the speaker intended.

If you are an effective listener and leader, you will use the time variance to anticipate what the speaker will say next, analyze the speaker's message, search for meaning, and review previous points the speaker made to reinforce their ideas.

Listening is an acquired skill – often forgotten in our rush to maintain our hectic and increasingly global business endeavors. Good listening skills pay off. Conversely, poor listening skills have measurable results, which are negative personally and professionally.

Three Factors Affect Your Ability to Listen

1. **Motivation is a significant element of successful listening.** Your comprehension improves if you are interested in the topic, if the message itself is interesting and entertaining, or if you know you are going to be tested on the content of the message.

2. **Organization of the message directly affects your comprehension of the message.** If you can organize and structure a message as you listen to it, you will understand more. Those speakers who deliver the message best can help by presenting it in an organized manner.

3. **Environment factors influence comprehension.** Have you ever let yourself be distracted by external noise, excessive fidgeting by the speaker, poor lighting, and a host of other distractions or problems that can arise? Effective listeners learn to compensate for these distractions.

Good Listening means ACTIVE Involvement

Content and attitude are two important elements in any verbal message that you, as an active listener, must try to understand.

Author **Stephen Covey** says in his *The Seven Habits of Highly Effective People*: *"…you must listen with your eyes and with your heart. You must listen for feeling, as well as for meaning. You must listen for behavior. You must use your right brain as well as your left. You sense, you intuit, you feel…"*

Probing questions will help you improve your listening skills. Watch for visual or soft sound cues. Voice inflection, the use of …pauses, and the speaker's expressions, posture, hand gestures, eye movements and breathing can provide you with help to understand the message. The following are excerpts from my Active Listening series.

ACTIVE LISTENING SKILLS

Good listening skills are important to any organization and specifically to your leadership or personal career! Listening is an essential part of the communication process in how we obtain, process, and pass along information. It is an acquired skill applied by top performing leaders to help their teams grow and succeed.

The communication process incorporates four basic elements:

- Reading
- Writing
- Speaking
- **Listening**

To begin, it is important to understand the true essence of listening. Someone once told me that, *"listening is to hearing, what reading is to seeing"*. Webster's defines hearing as, *"to perceive or apprehend using the ear"*. Listening on the other hand is defined as, *"to pay attention to sound – to hear with thoughtful attention"*.

How can good listening skills or lack of these skills impact your life, family or career? **The consequences of poor listening skills include:**

- Lower productivity and morale
- Lost sales
- Unhappy clients
- Increased costs
- Lost profits
- Less effective use of time, people, and resources
- Relationship breakdowns and personality clashes
- Accidents
- Production breakdowns and wasted time and effort

Good listening skills:

- Help improve relationships
- Minimize serious misunderstandings
- Leverage use of time, people, and resources
- Improve communications between co-workers, management, suppliers, and clients

Learn to question effectively so you can be a more successful listener. Don't be afraid to actively get the information you need to ensure you've effectively heard and clearly understood the message. This part is your responsibility. Effective communication is a partnership between speaker and listener to ensure the information is accurately transmitted and received.

Why don't we listen if we know the negative consequences and positive benefits? Here are a few ideas gleaned from class discussions over the years.

- Listening is hard work, concentrating on the other person and actively focusing our energies to hear and understand what they say.
- We have enormous competition for our attention in today's society with radio, TV, movies, written material, and the Internet clamoring for our time. We are overloaded daily with stimuli we must process and prioritize just to survive.
- We jump in and interrupt, because we 'THINK' we know what the other person is going to say, thereby depriving them of being heard out in full.

- The listening GAP (listening capabilities at 400-500 words per minute compared to speaking at 100-250 words per minute) between the speed of thought and speech allows us to jump to conclusions, fill in the time with daydreaming, form a reply or rebuttal, or work on other projects mentally.
- Lack of formal training, even though we do much more listening than reading or speaking. Many untrained listeners retain less than 25% of what they hear. This means effectively that 75% of what we hear may be distorted or forgotten.

We tend to listen at one of several attentive levels. While they tend to overlap or interchange, it is important that we be aware of these various levels.

- **Unconscious** listener: doesn't even hear the speaker. A blank look or glazed eyes, faking attention, nervous gestures, or constant interruptions accompany this level.
- **Superficial** listener: hears the sounds but doesn't understand the meaning or intent of the words. This person is too busy preparing their next statement to really listen and is quite easily distracted by their environment.
- **Evaluative** listener: is trying to hear what is being said, but again not really understanding what is being meant or the intent of the speaker. More concerned with content than feelings, focusing on logic and responding to the message by evaluating the words delivered, ignoring the vocal intonation, facial expression, or body language which gives us the broader, more accurate message.
- **ACTIVE** listener: is a powerful listener focusing on understanding the speaker's point of view, paying attention to the thoughts and feelings in addition to the words.

Active listening means refraining from judging the speaker's message, suspending for the moment our own feelings and thoughts to get to the speaker's intent and message. ACTIVE listening is hard work, as it requires our attention and concentration, as well as mental and emotional processing.

Techniques to help you 'focus'

The following techniques will help you focus and concentrate while listening. They will also help you counteract distractions.

- Deep breathing: whenever you feel like interrupting the speaker, take a deep breath… and listen! It works… if you're breathing in, you can't interrupt, can you?
- Make a 'conscious decision' to LISTEN by paying attention and looking for interesting items in the conversation. Mentally paraphrase what the speaker is saying. By putting it in your own words you keep concentrating and help to prevent yourself from daydreaming. By echoing, evaluating, rephrasing, anticipating, and reviewing what the speaker is saying, you help yourself to concentrate on the speaker, not yourself.
- Maintain eye contact. Your ears will often follow where your eyes lead. Acknowledge the speaker by maintaining eye contact, smiling, nodding, leaning forward, facing the speaker, or using appropriate facial or body gestures to project a positive response.
- Clarify points by asking questions or restating the information, to ensure you've gotten it accurately. You may even use verbal strokes, like "really", "Hmmm", "go on" to help draw out the speaker.
- Be actively involved in research! By research I mean clarifying a message, enlarging on a topic, getting the speaker to change conversational direction, or prompting then to tell you more. This allows us to support the speaker by reinforcing particular parts of their talk.

Listening is part of a two-way flow of communication, which facilitates a meeting of the minds and helps make the speaker feel more comfortable and able to open up.

- **Exercise emotional control** instead of focusing on the provocative aspects of a speaker's appearance, accent, vocal tone, vocabulary, or style. If we don't do this, we may miss the true substance and meaning of the speaker's message.
- **Learn how to recognize and redirect negative emotional reactions.** Pause to delay your reaction, find common ground (i.e. what you have in common) instead of focusing on differences and learn how to visualize yourself relaxed and calm. It helps!

Popular research has shown that only 7 to 10% of the message, the meaning, is carried through the words we use. Close to 90% of the message is conveyed through the vocal and visual presentation channels.

Someone once told me, *"In speaking…YOU are the message!"* This would be true as a leader too! This is not too far off the mark, if we consider the weight our audience places on the way we speak and in how we present our message, compared to the words we use.

Three Methods. There are three methods which will help you actively listen to the content of a speaker's message and prevent yourself from drifting off.
1. 'Comparing' between what is fact and what is opinion, between the positives and the negatives, between the pros and cons, and between the advantages and disadvantages.
2. Listening to hear 'if' the speaker is 'consistent' with his or her own material. 'Sequencing' is essentially listening for priority or logical order. Listen for transitional words like, 1st, 2nd, 3rd, or next.
3. 'Indexing' by taking written or mental note of the major idea or topic, the key points as discussed or outlined, and the sub-points or reasons and supporting points brought out by the speaker. Again, listen for those transitional words.

Make sure you hear and understand the words being used. This can be a major source of miscommunication between people, more so with our blended cultural backgrounds and experience. In North America, we have about 500 or so more commonly used English words with a potential for over 14,000 connotations or definitions. Perhaps it is possible for us to misunderstand the use of a particular word in conversation?

Listen in 'context' and check it out if you're not sure. Don't react emotionally or negatively to a word – it might not be meant in that manner. Check it out first – then act if necessary. This can be the most productive business building/ customer service tip I can give you.

Learn to listen for the connotation, which is essentially what the word means through suggestion, context, or implication, rather than definition, which is focused on the dictionary meaning.

When we assign a different meaning to a word than the speaker we miss or bypass the communication process. It takes concentration to ensure we hear and understand.

We can develop an ACTIVE LISTENING ATTITUDE, but it takes work and reinforcement. When we decide listening is just as powerful as speech, we begin to give our listening skills more attention.

Active Listening:

- Saves time
- Fewer mistakes
- Less misunderstandings
- **Reduces customer or employee turnover and frustration**

- Helps us in our interpersonal relationships
- Allows us to suspend judgment for the moment
- Allows us to really communicate by hearing what is said, before we respond

When we truly believe that we can learn from everyone we meet, we begin to realize our listening skills are vitally important and worthwhile. It is worth the effort. This excerpt is originally from a special college program in **Applied Communication Skills.** It was taught by the author in Vancouver, BC for many years and was a 'foundation for effective presentations' due to its parallel leadership lessons and its applied techniques in helping understand and focus on our audiences and those with whom we interact or lead.

Your listening skills will prove invaluable in Q &A periods, reading the moods of those who are listening to your presentations, and in getting the information you need to effectively present your views and projects. They will help you in your relationships with family, friends, co-workers, employees, team members, and community groups. Additionally, as a part of effective communication skills, your improved listening will help set you apart in your career advancement. Leaders use active listening skills as a bridge to connection with their teams.

"Most importantly when you ask 'strategic' questions that draw out your clients and actually listen to them you will be more successful in selling them. They will tell you what you can do to earn their business. In addition, when you keep listening to prospects and current clients you will hear ideas that might even open new markets. Listening works!"

Not always retail in focus

Our patient, an 80-year-old woman, with terminal cancer, would never return to her home of over 40 years. You could sense her obvious distress at leaving her beloved home. Her husband put his hand on my shoulder and asked us to please take extra special care of the love of his life. We assured him that we understood how precious she was to him and promised that we would treat her like gold. He thanked us with tears in his eyes. As we wheeled her outside on the stretcher, we paused to allow her a final look at her home. She quietly took a 'picture of the heart'. Then we used her cell phone to take a digital picture for her. She smiled her appreciation as we loaded her into the ambulance. Calls like this are one of the reasons that I became an E.M.T. © *Corinne Clarke*

Success Keys from Rubbermaid

Rubbermaid is a successful company, generating 2.3 billion in retail sales. Not bad for a company who creates consumable products and take-for-granted ones for a multitude of uses.

Rubbermaid in their own words seek to *"Master the mundane"*.

They create storage products for the house, the garage, and the patio, anywhere something that needs to be durable, waterproof, and cost effective. You might even find some of their products in your office.

Their aim in creating these 'mundane' products is to promote, **"Consumer delight!"** They apply the **5 Ts** in their creative design and discussion process:

- **Trends:** Be aware of what is happening in the world.
- **Teams:** Harness the power of applied teamwork toward a focused goal.
- **Training:** Offer training to equip your teams to succeed.
- **Technology:** Acquire and learn technology to make what you do easier and to expand your ability to be creative and innovative.
- **Creative Tension:** Tension can be a good thing if applied creatively. Feed the process!

They even have **Trend Messengers** whose role it is to gather information from around the world around them and share their observations with the rest of their team. As managers, we can learn from their success. They've developed **'Seven success keys or operating principles'**, which have helped them reach their present level of success and will, no doubt, continue to do so.

1) **Cross-functional teams** are more reliably productive.
2) **Oversight teams**, drawn from the Company's top executives, supervise every business unit.
3) **Companywide business councils** focus on performance and innovation in such business practices as marketing and design.
4) **Scrutinize market trends** by keeping close watch on surface action and digging well beneath the surface for what customers are buying or would buy.
5) **Don't waste time on run-of-the-mill research.** Look for a need, impact, and invest the necessary dollars to make a difference.

6) **Impose creative tension**; inspire their people to come up with 'fresh' solutions to new tasks in new environments.
7) **Offer every kind of training** but leave it to individual associates to take advantage of it.

Consider the following:

- Can you learn from this successful creator of home, garage, and industrial products?
- Can you, like Rubbermaid, investigate the world around you and see opportunities to expand what you offer your clients, your team, and grow to the next level? My guess would be yes!
- Are you applying, or can you apply, some of these operating principles in your organization?
- What would be the response from your team if you did?
- Would they be more creative and able to explore opportunities for growth and innovation in your process, your products, and your services?
- What do you have to lose?
- When will you start this process?

What future do you want to experience? Make the decision to visualize and **Create Your Future** – the one you want! (www.SuccessPublications.ca)

Engagement is a secret weapon in a competitive market

"People want this level of engagement from the companies with which they do business ... even the best of what formerly passed for good customer service is no longer enough. You have to be no less than a customer concierge, doing everything you can to make every one of your customers feel acknowledged, appreciated, and heard. You have to make them feel special, just like when your great-grandmother walked into Butcher Bob's shop or bought her new hat and you need to make people who aren't your customers wish they were. Social media gives businesses the tools to do that for the first time in a scalable way.

It's very logical: There is proven ROI in doing whatever you can to turn your customers into advocates for your brand or business. The way to create advocates is to offer superior customer service."

Gary Vaynerchuk, quoted from '*The Thank You Economy*'

Service and Teach to Reach!

If you are serious about offering value-added service and meeting the needs of our customers, you need to explore some different avenues to help them solve or resolve their problems. You need to find creative ways to let them know who you are, what you do, and where you are to help them. Here are just a few areas that successful businesses have used in their efforts to assist them. I've been able to apply many of them to better serve my clients, audiences, and readers. Some of these will lend themselves to your business.

Showroom or in-store seminars

If your product or service lends itself to being more effectively used using different applications, holding an in-house session is a great idea. How can you adapt or change your situation to be able to offer this service to your customers? *BTW: This is how I started my speaking career.*

In-house or client newsletters

Keeping in touch and sharing information on how to better use your products or services or what's happening in your industry is a great way to serve. With new software programs, this is increasingly easier to accomplish. I'd suggest doing these 3 to 4 times a year at first, so you don't promise what you can't deliver. Keep it simple and conversational. Keep the focus on WIIFM – what's in it for me!

Write it from their perspective if you would truly serve them. It can even be done as an e-letter and sent via the Internet. When will you start? What will you call it? Send me a copy… **bob@ideaman.net … I'd love to see it!**

Send (relevant) stories to local media

Become a source of relevant information to your community by taking the risk of sending items of interest to their readers to the media. Keeping people informed about newsworthy developments is a customer service activity. How can you do this in your area? Share on social media as well.

Write a booklet, workbook, or book

If you have built a solid reputation or a depth of experience in your field, perhaps you can add value to your service or business by taking the time to write a few thoughts. It doesn't have to be a work of art, just valuable and easily read. *It has worked well for me.* ☺

Mall shows, trade, or home shows

A great opportunity to provide a needed service to potential customers. It's a bit of work, but it will pay off in the long run. Does your firm or product lend itself to this type of instruction and marketing? Check out opportunities in your area to better serve your customers, by sharing your knowledge and exhibiting what you provide to the market. Is there a mall show in your area that you can enter? How about a display at a local bank or other location?

Continuing education or guest lecturer

This is how I started and eventually this outpouring of my training as a professional kitchen designer allowed me to teach my fellow designers and potential customers alike. Later, I had the opportunity to expand my areas of instruction into the areas of time management, creativity, leadership, sales, and, of course, Customer Service. This has allowed me to travel the globe. What is it you know that would be 'teachable' and of value to potential customers? What is stopping you from taking this step?

Become a media resource

Contact your local media and let them know you'd be willing to act as a source if something comes up within your area of expertise. Often, they are looking for local or national responses to breaking stories. If they know you and your expertise, you might be called on to respond or comment as an industry 'expert.' What can you be an 'expert' on? Make a commitment to let them know! This is another area where you can leverage on social media.

Other ideas (such as on-line social media)

Using Twitter, Facebook, LinkedIn have opened conversations with new clients over the years. Contribute ideas and engage with people as a value provider. It works. I'm sure as you read this, other ideas have crossed your mind. Take a moment to jot them down here.

"We are the architects and builders helping people build a better life. We put windows into their thinking to help them see and think more clearly. We are doctors giving a shot of laughter to heavy hearts. We are chefs and dieticians, selecting the right ingredients and serving up appetizing food for thought. We are salesmen of ideas and ideals. We are farmers planting seeds and fertilizing minds. We are trainers, evangelists, and much more..."
Charley 'Tremendous' Jones

Turning a Winning Proposal into a Loser

Perhaps your client is found and serviced by on-site visits and sales calls. Perhaps your initial connection is via a phone call or from a website. When you have a chance to present your services or an offer to purchase your products it is important to follow through. Too many salespeople and negotiators have done just the opposite and ended up losing the deal. They have learned how to turn a winning proposal into a loser. To tell you how to accomplish that, **we'll describe some of the ways that winning proposals are often turned into losers**, and what you can do to avoid these losing situations.

Just 'Mail/Email It' To Them

Having asked you for a formal written proposal, some prospects will then ask you to mail it to them so they can 'look it over' and make their decision. Or worse, they set up an appointment for you to deliver your proposal in person, and then cancel the appointment on short notice and ask you to just mail/email it.

So, what's wrong with that? If your proposal is so good, why can't it stand on its own merits without your help? **Here are a few reasons why not:**

- Few prospects will bother to read your carefully crafted proposal from cover to cover. They skip around or jump directly to the end; they lose the story flow that you have so carefully built.
- No matter how carefully your proposal has been written, it can't include everything the prospect needs to hear – the verbal amplifications, the case study stories of how you solved similar problems for other customers – nor can a written document pause for effect or add emphasis in just the right place.
- Your written proposal can't read the prospect's body language for you, it can't answer questions, and it can't handle objections. If the prospect is reading it and hits a point of confusion or disagreement, who is going to help them get past that point of concern? **Customer service is being there to help the client fully understand it!**
- You don't know who is looking at your proposal. In addition to your primary contact, is someone who has a vested interest in finding fault with your solution reading it (they love the present solution and don't want you to make waves)?
- If the prospect does read your proposal and likes it, you're not there to seize the moment and ask for the order.

If you can possibly avoid it, never just mail your proposal to the prospect. Offer one or more of these reasons why you must present it in person:

- The written proposal tells only part of the story. I need to explain a few points, or they won't make sense.
- I need to show you some examples (slides, a video, etc.).
- I know you will like what we have to offer, but there are others in your company who will have technical questions that need to be answered before they throw their support behind this decision.
- I have prepared 'several' alternative approaches, with different specifications and pricing. I'll need to ask you a few questions and then explain the pros and cons for each of them.

Skip the Agenda

You've heard it before: *"Tell them what you're going to tell them, tell them, and tell them what you told them."* Yet, many salespeople launch into their proposal presentation, omitting the first of these three steps.

Here's the problem – chances are very good that since your last meeting with the prospect, something has changed:

- A competitor has raised a new issue, causing the prospect to change his mind about what he wants.
- Some new business pressure has caused the prospect to change his mind.
- Someone in the 'Prospect Company' has a new requirement.
- Nothing has really changed, but as the decision point draws near, cold feet about making a decision cause the prospect to rethink his position on something.

At the beginning of your proposal presentation, hand out a copy of your agenda for the meeting or display it on a white board or easel. Talk through what you will cover, and then ask: **Are there any other points you would like to cover today?** Whatever the prospect says, write it down on your agenda and make sure you cover it.

Hand Out Your Proposal at The Beginning

Particularly when presenting your proposal to a committee, a sure way to get into trouble is to hand everyone a copy with the intention of going through it together. When you do this, some things are likely to happen:

- At least one person will immediately search for the pricing, particularly if they think you are too high. Once they find it, count on them to shake their head and point out the huge total to the person sitting next to them. Never mind that they don't yet understand what they get for that price; they already don't like your proposal.
- Meanwhile, some other 'small-minded' individual will flip through the pages to determine how well you handled their pet feature, whether or not it is really important to the decision-maker. Then, out of the blue, they will start asking questions like: *"How come on page 32 you talk about left-handed green widget brackets when we have always used right-handed aqua ones?"*
- Even if no one flips ahead, an unlikely case, you want everyone's attention focused on you and the compelling story you are telling, not with their noses buried in the book.

Your 'winning' strategy for proposal delivery is to explain like this:

- In a little while I will give each of you a copy of our formal written proposal. But first, what we will do is go through the highlights of our proposal and how it will address your needs.
- Then, use videos, PowerPoint, a white board, or just your own, well-rehearsed story-telling abilities to communicate the essence of your proposal.
- Once you have secured agreement that you correctly understand the prospect's needs, have a solution that makes sense to them, and have answered all their questions about your proposed solution, you're ready to hand out the written proposal.
- Since they already know the big stuff, you can then go directly to the pricing, implementation schedule, and other finishing details before asking for the order.

Ignore Lesser Players

Whether the key decision-maker comes alone or with an entourage, there are almost always other people involved in the decision. Most of them do not have the power to say: 'Yes' but many of them may have the power to say: 'No'.

Some of the best no-sayers are attorneys, accountants, engineers, and bookkeepers – anybody in a position to whine about some small flaw in your proposal that will make their life more difficult. Before presenting your proposal, make sure you know who these decision-influencers are and that you have reached out to every one of them to arrest their worst fears.

Introduce Untested Surprises in Your Proposal Presentation

Presentation of your formal proposal should be a confirmation of everything you have previously discussed with the prospect, plus a few minor details. Your goal is to have a proposal presentation so solid that the prospect has no good reason not to accept it today.

If your proposal presentation introduces major new ideas that you have not previously tested on the prospect, the likely result is that you will be at least somewhat off the mark. Then, you are forced to resubmit your proposal later, reflecting your new understanding of what the prospect wants. You've lost momentum, and you've given the competition an opportunity to offer a winning solution first.

Prior to your formal proposal presentation, review any new ideas with the decision-maker and talk through all major ideas you will present to be sure you are on track. Ask questions about any open issues and, if necessary, fax or email a draft of critical specifications or other details beforehand for confirmation.

Now you know different ways to scuttle your beautiful proposal. Avoid these mistakes and all you need to do is deliver your compelling story of **why you and your company:**

1. Understand this prospect's needs better than anyone else.
2. Have products and services which are a glove-tight fit for those needs.
3. Are going to knock yourselves out to exceed the prospect's expectations in every area, today and for years into the future.

Landing the deal or getting the order is so more than just making an offer or dropping off a proposal as we see from these points. It is also a visible proof of your willingness to be there for them. It is also another step in building a solid, long-term, profitable relationship with them.

In today's competitive market you cannot afford to let your guard down for a moment. There is always someone hungrier and more willing to go the extra mile. Make sure it is you and your team!

Gee that sounds like customer service to me, which is why I included this section. If you are to succeed, you must go the extra mile – you must go the distance. Anything less is shoddy customer service and is definitely not value-added.

Needing Others

Many living things need each other to survive. If you have ever seen a Colorado aspen tree, you may have noticed that it does not grow alone. Aspens are found in clusters or groves.

The reason is that the aspen sends up new shoots from the roots. In a small grove, all of the trees may actually be connected by their roots!

Giant California redwood trees may tower 300 feet into the sky. It would seem that they would require extremely deep roots to anchor them against strong winds.

But we're told that their roots are actually quite shallow – in order to capture as much surface water as possible. And they spread in all directions, intertwining with other redwoods.

Locked together in this way, all the trees support each other in wind and storms. Like the aspen, they never stand alone. They need one another to survive.

People, too, are connected by a system of roots. We are born to family and learn early to make friends. We are not meant to survive long without others.

And like the redwood, we need to hold one another up. When pounded by the sometimes, vicious storms of life, we need others to support and sustain us.

Have you been going it alone? Maybe it's time to let someone else help hold you up for a while. Or perhaps someone needs to hang on to you.

Author Unknown

Visit: www.SuccessPublications.ca/BusinessSuccess-Tips.html for special business building success tips, just for you.

Bob's B.E.S.T. publications

Bob is a *prolific* author who has been capturing and sharing his wisdom and experience in print and electronic formats for the past fifteen plus years. In addition to the following publications, several of them best sellers, he has written for consumer, corporate, professional associations, trade, and on-line publications. He has been engaged to write and assist on publications by other best-selling writers and successful companies. His publications are listed to give you an idea of the scope and topics he writes about. Bob's **B**usiness **E**nhancement **S**uccess **T**ools.

Leadership, business, and career development series

- **Running TOO Fast** (8th edition 2022)
- **Legacy of Leadership** (3rd edition 2022)
- **Make ME Feel Special!** (6th edition 2022)
- **Why Didn't I 'THINK' of That?** (6th edition 2022)
- **Speaking for Success!** (9th edition 2022)
- **THINK Beyond the First Sale** (3rd edition 2022)
- **Prepare Yourself to Win!** (3rd edition 2017)
- **The early years… 1998-2009 – A Tip of the Hat collection** (2020)
- **The saga continues… 2010-2019 – A Tip of the Hat collection** (2020)
- **Sales Success Secrets -2 volume set** (2022)

Bob's Mini-book success series

- **The Courage to Lead!** (4th edition 2017)
- **Creative Conflict** (3rd edition 2017)
- **Get to YES!** (3rd edition 2017)
- **THINK Before You Ink!** (3rd edition 2017)
- **Running to Win!** (2nd edition 2017)

- **How to Generate More Sales** (4th edition 2017)
- **Unleash your Business Potential** (3rd edition 2017)
- **Maximize Meetings** (new for 2019)
- **Learn to Listen** (2nd edition 2017)
- **Creativity Counts!** (updated 2016)
- **Create Your Future!** (3rd edition 2017)

Bob's Pocket Wisdom series – *print and epub*

- **Pocket Wisdom for Speakers** (updated 2019)
- **Pocket Wisdom for Leaders – Power of One!** (updated 2019)

Kindle Shorts (2017-2020) series - *more to come in 2023*

- **SPEAK!**
- **LEAD!**
- **SERVE!**
- **CREATE!**
- **CONFLICT!**
- **TIME!**
- **SUCCEED!**
- **WRITE ON!**

Co-authored books created by Bob

- Quantum Success – 3 volume series (2006) (to be updated 2023)
- **In The Company of Leaders** (95th anniversary Edition 2019)
- Foundational Success (2nd Edition 2013)
- **PIVOT to Present** (2020) to assist in speaking virtually

Visit: www.SuccessPublications.ca for more information on Bob's publications and other success resources.

Want to empower your team? Ask about our volume discount packages for *'Make ME Feel Special!'* Write us at: bob@ideaman.net

Thanks for reading 'Make ME Feel Special!'

Each time I prepare to step on the stage; each time I sit down to write or in this case to re-write, I am challenged to deliver something that will be of use-it-now value to my audience/reader.

- I ask myself, *"If I was reading this, what value would I be looking for?"*
- As well as *"Why is this relevant to me, today?"*

These two questions help to keep me focused and clear on my objectives. They help to remind me to dig into my experiences, stories, examples, and research to provide solid information that will be of benefit and help our readers, when they apply it, succeed. That can be an exciting challenge!

I trust we have done that for you in this updated primer on enhanced business success. *'Make ME Feel Special!'* is my attempt to capture some of the lessons learned first-hand from observing and working with some tremendously effective leaders, retailers, service providers, and business owners.

Bob 'Idea Man' Hooey
2011 Spirit of CAPS recipient
www.ideaman.net
www.BobHooey.training
www.HaveMouthWillTravel.com

Connect with me on:

- **Facebook:** www.facebook.com/bob.hooey
- **LinkedIn:** www.linkedin.com/in/canadianideamanbobhooey
- **YouTube:** www.youtube.com/ideamanbob
- **Smashwords:** www.smashwords.com/profile/view/Hooey
- **Follow me on Twitter:** @IdeamanHooey
- **Snail mail:** Box 10, Egremont, Alberta, T0A0Z0, CANADA
- **Amazon:** www.amazon.com/Bob-Idea-Man-Hooey/e/B00FACOHNY

About the author

Bob 'Idea Man' Hooey is a charismatic, confident leader, corporate trainer, inspiring facilitator, Emcee, prolific author, and award-winning motivational keynote speaker on leadership, creativity, success, business innovation, and enhancing team performance.

Using personal stories drawn from rich experience, he challenges his audiences to engage his **Ideas At Work!** – To act on what they hear, with clear, innovative building-blocks and field-proven success techniques to increase their effectiveness. Bob challenges them to hone specific 'success skills' critical to their personal and professional advancement.

Bob outlines real-life, results-based, innovative ideas personally drawn from 29 plus years of rich leadership experience in retail, construction, small business, entrepreneurship, manufacturing, association, consulting, community service, and commercial management.

Bob's conversational, often humorous, professional, and sometimes-provocative style continues to inspire and challenge his audiences across North America. Bob's motivational, innovative, challenging, and practical **Ideas At Work!** have been successfully applied by thousands of leaders and professionals across the globe. Busy man – productive man!

Bob is a frequent contributor to North American consumer, corporate, association, trade, and on-line publications on leadership, success, employee motivation and training; as well as creativity and innovative problem solving, priority and time management, and effective customer service. He is the inspirational author of 30 plus publications, including several best-selling, print, e-books, reader style e-pubs, and a Pocket Wisdom series.

Visit: **www.SuccessPublications.ca** for more information.

Retired, award winning kitchen designer, Bob Hooey, CKD-Emeritus was one of only 75 Canadian designers to earn this prestigious certification by the US based National Kitchen and Bath Association.

In December 2000, Bob was given a special CAPS National Presidential award **"...for his energetic contribution to the advancement of CAPS and his living example of the power of one"** in addition to being elected to the CAPS National Board (Canadian Association of Professional Speakers). He has been recognized by the National Speakers Association and other groups for his leadership contributions.

Bob is a co-founder and a Past President of the CAPS Vancouver Chapter and served as 2012 President of the CAPS Edmonton Chapter. He is a member of the NSA-Arizona Chapter, a charter member of the Canadian Association of Professional Speakers, as well as the Global Speakers Federation. He retired (December 2013) as a Trustee from the CAPS Foundation following a successful 5-year term.

In 1998, Toastmasters International recognized Bob **"...for his professionalism and outstanding achievements in public speaking"**. That August in Palm Desert, California Bob became the 48th speaker in the world to be awarded this prestigious professional level honor as an **Accredited Speaker**. He has been inducted into their Hall of Fame on numerous occasions for his leadership contributions.

Bob has been honoured by the United Nations Association of BC (1993) and received the **CANADA 125 award** (1992) for his ongoing leadership contributions to the community. In 1998, Bob joined 3 other men to sail a 65-foot gaff rigged schooner from Honolulu, Hawaii to Kobe, Japan, barely surviving a 'baby' typhoon enroute.

In November 2011 Bob was awarded the Spirit of CAPS at their annual convention, becoming the 11th speaker to earn this prestigious CAPS National award. Visit: www.ideaman.net/SoC.htm

Bob loves to travel, and his speaking and writing have allowed him to visit 46 countries so far. Perhaps your organization would like to bring Bob in to share a few ideas with your leaders and teams around the globe.

Visit: **www.HaveMouthWillTravel.com** for more information.

Copyright and Credits

Make ME Feel Special! – *Idea-rich customer service strategies!*
(6th edition updated 2022)

By Bob 'Idea Man' Hooey, Accredited Speaker, 2011 Spirit of CAPS recipient. Prolific author of 30 plus business, leadership, sales, and career success publications

© Copyright 1998-2022 Bob 'Idea Man' Hooey

All rights reserved worldwide
No part of this publication may be retained, copied, sold, rented or loaned, transmitted, reproduced, broadcast, performed, or distributed in any such medium, or by any means, nor stored in any computer or distributed over any network without permission in writing from the publisher and/or author. Care has been taken to trace ownership of copyright material contained in this volume. The publisher will gladly receive information that will allow him to rectify any reference or credit line in subsequent editions. Segments of this publication were originally published as articles and/or parts of other books and program materials and are included here by permission of the publishers and authors. All pictures and graphics are royalty free or used under license. Unattributed quotations are by Bob 'Idea Man' Hooey

This book by **Bob 'Idea Man' Hooey** was originally published in 1998 as *'Secrets of Effective Customer Service'* and has been updated numerous times over the years. It was rewritten and renamed *'Make ME Feel Special!' Idea-rich customer service strategies* for 2014, updated in 2017 and 2022.

Cover design: **Wendy** (www.fiverr.com/craftarc)
Photos of Bob: **Dov Friedman**, www.photographybyDov.com
              Irene Gaudet, www.VitrakCreative.com
              Frédéric Bélot, www.fredericbelot.fr/fr
Editorial, layout and design: **Irene Gaudet**, Vitrak Creative Services

ISBN 13: 9781790300921

Printed in the United States 10 9 8 7 6 5 4 3 2 1

Success Publications
Leadership success series
Box 10, Egremont, AB T0A 0Z0
www.successpublications.ca
Creative office: 1-780-736-0009

Acknowledgements, credits, and disclaimers

As with each of my books, a very special dedication of this piece of myself, to the two people who meant the most to me, my folks **Ron and Marge Hooey**. Sadly, both my parents left this earthly realm in 1999. I still miss our time together and your encouragement and love. I was blessed with the two of you in my life.

To my inspiring wife and professional proofreader and publications coach, **Irene Gaudet**, who loves, encourages, and supports me in my quest to continue sharing my **Ideas At Work!** across the world. Thank you seems so inadequate for your timely work in helping make my writing and my client service better! I love the time we spend together!

My thanks to the many people who have encouraged me in my growth as a leader, speaker, and engaging trainer in each area of expertise including *'Make ME Feel Special!'*

- To my colleagues and friends in the National Speakers Association **(NSA)**, the Canadian Association of Professional Speakers **(CAPS)**, and the Global Speakers Federation **(GSF)** who continually challenge me to strive for success and increased excellence.
- To my friend, **Lindsay Adams, CSP Global** for insights and support.
- To my many friends and family around the world, to whom I owe an unpayable debt of gratitude for your investment, encouragement, time, and support when I was just starting down this path; and oh, so rough around the edges. To those who shared stories included here.
- **To my great audiences, leaders, students, coaching clients, and readers across the globe** who share their experiences and enjoyment of my work. Your positive and supportive feedback encourages me to keep working on additional programs and success publications like this updated version. My experience with you creates the foundation for additional real-life experiences I can take from the stage to the page, the classroom to the boardroom.
- My thanks to a *select* few friends for your ongoing support and 'constructive' abuse. You know who you are. ☺

Disclaimer

We have not attempted to cite all the authorities and sources consulted in the preparation of this book. To do so would require much more space than is available. The list would include departments of various governments, libraries, industrial institutions, periodicals, and many individuals. Inspiration was drawn from many sources, including other books by the author, in this updated creation of ***'Make ME Feel Special'***

This book is written and designed to provide information on more effective use of your time in attracting and retaining clients, and as a life and leadership enhancement guide. It is sold with the 'explicit' understanding that the publisher and/or the author(s) are **not** engaged in rendering legal, accounting, or other professional services. If legal or other expert assistance is required, the services of a competent professional in your geographic area should be sought.

It is not the purpose of this book to reprint all the information that is otherwise available. Its primary purpose is to complement, amplify, and supplement other books and reference materials already available. You are encouraged to search out and study all the available material, learn as much as possible, and tailor the information to your individual needs. This will help to enhance your success in being a more effective leader or professional.

Every effort has been made to make this book as complete and as accurate as possible within the scope of its focus. However, there may be mistakes, both typographical and in content or attribution. Care has been taken to trace ownership of copyright material contained in this volume. The publisher will gladly receive information that will allow him to rectify any reference or credit line in subsequent editions. This book should be used only as a general guide and not as the ultimate source of information. Furthermore, this book contains information that is current only up to the date of publication.

The purpose of ***'Make ME Feel Special!'*** is to educate and entertain; perhaps to inform and to inspire. It is certainly to challenge its readers to learn and apply its secrets and tips, to challenge them to enhance their skills and leverage their time to create more productive outcomes within their respective businesses in better serving their clients and customers.

The author and publisher shall have **neither** liability **nor** responsibility to any person or entity with respect to any loss or damage caused, or alleged to have been caused, directly or indirectly, by the information contained in this book.

What they say about Bob 'Idea Man' Hooey

As I travel across North America, and more recently around the globe, sharing my **Ideas At Work!** I am fortunate to get feedback and comments from my audiences and colleagues. These comments come from people who have been touched, challenged, or simply enjoyed themselves in one of my sessions. **I'd love to come and share some ideas with your organization and teams.**

"I've known Bob for several years and follow his activities in business with interest. I originally met Bob when he spoke for a Rotary Leadership Institute and got to know him better when he came to Vladivostok, Russia to speak to our leadership. **When you spoke, I thought you were one of us because you talked about our challenges just like yours.** *You could understand the others, which makes you a great speaker!"* **Andrey Konyushok**, *Rotary International District 2225 Governor 2012-2013, far eastern Russia*

"I still get comments from people about your presentation. **Only a few speakers have left an impression that lasts that long.** *You hit a spot with the tourism people."* **Janet Bell**, *Yukon Economic Forums*

"We greatly appreciate **the energy and effort you put into researching and adapting your keynote to make it more meaningful to our member councils.** *Early feedback from our delegates indicates that this year's convention was one of our most successful events yet, and we thank you for your contribution to this success."* **Larry Goodhope**, *Executive Director Alberta Association of Municipal Districts and Counties*

"Thank you, Bob, it is **always a pleasure to see a true professional at work.** *You have made the name 'Speaker' stand out as a truism - someone who encourages people to examine their lives and make adjustments. The personal stories you shared with your audience made such a great impression on everyone.* **The comments indicated you hit people right where it is important - in their hearts.** *Each of those in your audience took away a new feeling of personal success and encouragement."* **Sherry Knight**, *Dimension Eleven Human Resources and Communications*

"Bob is one of those rare individuals who knows how to tackle obstacles in life to reach his dreams. He takes each as a learning **experience and stretches for more.** *His compassion and genuine interest in others, make him an exceptional coach."* **Cindy Kindret**, *Training Manager, Silk FM Radio*

"Without doubt, **I have gained immeasurable self-assurance.** Bob, your patience and your encouragement has been much appreciated. **I strongly recommend your course to anyone looking for self-improvement and professional development.**" **Jeannie Mura**, *Human Resources Chevron Canada*

"I am pleased to recommend Bob 'Idea Man' Hooey to any organization looking for a charismatic, confident speaker and seminar leader. I have seen Bob in action on several occasions, and he is ALWAYS on! Bob has the ability to grab his audience's attention and keep it. Quite simply, **if Bob is involved - your program or seminar is guaranteed to succeed.**" **Maurice Laving**, *Coordinator Training and Development, London Drugs*

"I have found **Bob's attention to detail** and his ability to fine tune his seminars to match the time frame and needs of the audience to be a valuable asset to our educational program." **Patsy Schell**, *Executive Director Surrey Chamber of Commerce*

"Great seeing you in Cancun and congratulations on a job well done. **The seminar was a great success! Your humorous and conversational style was a tremendous asset.** It is my sincere hope that we can be associated again at future seminars." **Donald MacPherson**, *Attorney at Law, Phoenix, Arizona*

"**What a great conference.** It was a great pleasure meeting with you at the Ritz Carlton, Cancun and I shall look forward to hopefully welcoming you and your family in Dublin, Ireland someday." **A. Paul Ryan**, *Petronva Corporation, Dublin, Ireland*

"Congratulations on the **Spirit of CAPS Award.** You have worked long and hard on behalf of CAPS …**helped many speakers including me** and richly deserve this award. Well done my friend." **Peter Legge**, **CSP, Hof, CPAE**

"I had the pleasure of hearing and watching Bob Hooey deliver a keynote speech several years ago, when he gave a presentation at a Toastmasters International Convention. **Bob impressed me greatly with his professionalism, energy, and ability to connect with his audience while giving them value.** I heartily recommend this talented speaker and 'Idea Man' to all who want to move to the next level." **Dr. Dilip Abayasekara, DTM, Accredited Speaker,** *Past President, Toastmasters International*

"I attended **Speaking for Success** in Edmonton. **The mark of a true leader is someone who will lay down their own pride to teach all they know to their potential successors.** To be taught by a man of his caliber was an honor whether you're a beginner like myself or a professional; the experience is well worth it! To Bob - it truly was an honor to meet you. Stay humble and enjoy the great success." **Samantha McLeod**

Engage Bob for your leaders and their teams

"I have been so excited working with Bob Hooey, as he has given inspiration and motivation to our leadership team members. Both at the Brick Warehouse – Alberta and at Art Van Furniture – Michigan; with his years of experience in working with business executives and his humorous and delightful packaging of his material, he makes learning with Bob a real joy. But most importantly, anyone who comes in contact with his material is the better for it."
Kim Yost, CEO Art Van Furniture (retired), former CEO The Brick

Motivate your teams, your employees, and your leaders to 'productively' grow and 'profitably' succeed!

- Protect your conference investment - leverage your training dollars.
- Enhance your professional career and sell more products and services.
- Equip and motivate your leaders and their teams to grow and succeed, 'even' in tough times!
- Leverage your time to enhance your skills, equip your teams, and better serve your clients.
- Leverage your leadership and investment of time to leave a significant legacy within your organization and life!

Call today to engage best-selling author, award winning, inspirational leadership keynote speaker, leader's success coach, and employee development trainer, **Bob 'Idea Man' Hooey** and his innovative, audience based, results-focused, **Ideas At Work!** for your next company, convention, leadership, staff, training, or association event. You'll be glad you did!

Call 1-780-736-0009 to connect with
Bob 'Idea Man' Hooey today!
Learn more about Bob at: www.ideaman.net

"There is no such thing as a self-made man or woman. You will reach your goals only with the help of others." George Shin. This is where the time you invest working with your individual team members pays amazing dividends.

Visit: www.SuccessPublications.ca/BusinessSuccess-Tips.html for special business building success tips, just for you.

Manufactured by Amazon.ca
Bolton, ON